ASSISTING MINISTERS HANDBOOK

By Ralph R. Van Loon
Edited by S. Anita Stauffer

Parish Life Press
Philadelphia

RESOURCES FOR PARISH LEADERS

RESOURCES FOR PARISH LEADERS

Designed by Philip V. Tascone

The bottom right cover photograph is by Joseph McGinty. The other three cover photographs are by Stan Sadowski.

Scripture quotations in this publication are from the *Revised Standard Version Common Bible*, copyrighted © 1973.

Quotations from the *Lutheran Book of Worship*, copyright 1978, and the *Lutheran Book of Worship Ministers Edition*, copyright 1978, are used by permission.

Quotations from the "Apology of the Augsburg Confession," *The Book of Concord*, are from the 1959 edition translated by Theodore G. Tappert and copyrighted by Fortress Press, Philadelphia, Pennsylvania.

2017J85 Printed in U.S.A. 13-900043

INTRODUCTION

S. Anita Stauffer

The priesthood of all believers, as taught in the New Testament (1 Peter 2:5), was vigorously stressed during the Reformation. Lutherans recognize that Holy Baptism is a kind of ordination rite for all the people of God, because Baptism unites each Christian to the life and mission of the church's High Priest, Jesus Christ. This baptismal incorporation into Christ's priesthood gives each Christian the priestly privilege of offering holy worship to God and also gives the priestly appointment of witnessing to Christ in our everyday calling. And each Christian does have a calling; Baptism assures us of that. Some members of the priesthood are called to be pastors, but not all members receive such a call. Some are called to be evangelists, but not all. Some are called to be teachers or musicians or artists or writers or administrators, but not all receive such calls.

Some members of the Christian priesthood are called to live out their baptismal ministries as engineers or doctors or plumbers or bus drivers or chefs or homemakers or accountants or politicians or construction workers. The church's priesthood has this kind of diversity so that God has a priest, a witness, at every level and in every sphere of human life.

Within the congregation, a similar kind of diversity can be found. Some members serve as church school teachers, some as ushers, acolytes, parish visitors, committee members, lectors, singers, members of the altar guild, musicians, and so on. Such a diversity of callings exists so that congregations have the "person power" needed to be a well-functioning part of God's holy church, the Body of Christ.

Lutherans have a high commitment to this understanding of the priesthood of all believers. Such a commitment has been forged by Holy Baptism, and it finds expression in the Christian's self-understanding of what it means to be a priest of Christ in the world and in the church. As priests, all Christians are linked together in a priesthood—a community of the anointed where all are bound together by Holy Baptism, its responsibility for service, and its divine promises of life and salvation. As members of this royal priesthood of all believers, Christians have been welded together by the Holy Spirit to form the baptized family of God, the household of faith, the community of the redeemed.

Every Lord's Day, that priestly family is called together by the Holy Spirit for an extraordinarily profound reunion. Assembling about the family Table to share the family Meal, the household of faith gathers each week for a consequential encounter with God and with other members of the priesthood. Each priest comes to that encounter to do what priests like most to do: to offer priestly sacrifices of praise and thanksgiving to God through the church's High Priest, Jesus the Christ. Each priest also comes to that encounter to receive the nourishment of Word and Sacrament, those indispensable gifts of grace which equip and motivate each Christian to do priesthood in the world.

It is this weekly encounter, this Word and Sacrament event, which serves as the focus for this handbook as it addresses liturgical leadership. Those who plan and lead this priestly reunion each Lord's Day will want to be aware of the nature and intent of corporate worship and to be aware of the unique identity of those who assemble to worship. That is a singularly significant assemblage. It is not *just* a congregation, not *just* a gathering of learners, not *just* an audience of supportive patrons. Those who gather to celebrate the liturgy of our Lord's death and resurrection bear upon their brows the mark of priesthood. Their baptismal ordination prompts them to assemble as a convocation of royal priests, come together to do the first and urgent business of Christian priesthood: to offer adoration to God and to grow in grace and usefulness.

As priests, all participate fully in the service. These are priests who have convened to *do* their liturgy, not to watch it being done by others for them. As priests, all worshipers are fully attentive and fully involved as the church's liturgy re-presents salvation history and directs the prayers and praises of the priesthood to God through Christ. All are engaged in this holy event of Word and Sacrament, though some priests will have particular leadership roles. For example, one priest, whom the church has called and ordained into the ministry of Word and Sacrament, presides over the liturgy as the representative of Christ. In such a role, the pastor serves in the stead and place of Christ (*Apology of the Augsburg Confession*, Articles VII and VIII). It is the task of the pastor as presiding minister to lead those parts of the liturgy which are associated most closely with Christ's earthly ministry:

Confession and Forgiveness
Apostolic Greeting
Salutation and Prayer of the Day
Sermon
The Prayers (concluding commendation)
The Peace
The Great Thanksgiving: Preface Dialog through Lord's Prayer
Benediction

Those parts of the church's liturgy which require the leadership of an ordained pastor, however, are only a portion of the service. It is the expectation of the church's rubrics that other members of the congregation, especially lay persons, lead those parts of the liturgy which do not require an ordained minister. In the *Lutheran Book of Worship*, these leadership roles are easily identified. The pastor who serves as the presiding minister leads those sections of the liturgy which are marked ; those sections which are marked , meaning assisting minister, may be led by lay persons. It is not appropriate for a lay person to lead those parts of the liturgy which are assigned to the presiding minister.

It is important to remember that the use of lay persons in liturgical leadership roles is not based on the notion that the pastor needs help. The church's decision to widen the range of lay liturgical roles springs from an awareness of the meaning of Baptism and the meaning of corporate worship. As members of the baptismal priesthood, all believers have liturgical assignments. All priests assemble around the Lord's Table every Lord's Day.

Since some of those priests possess special gifts, they are enlisted to use those gifts in particular ways when the priesthood convenes to praise God. "For as in one body we have many members, and all the members do not have the same function, so we, though many, are one body in Christ, and individually members one of another. Having gifts that differ according to the grace given to us, let us use them" (Romans 12:4–6a). Therefore, those priests who read well should be encouraged to use that gift by serving as lectors. Those who have the gift of singing should serve as cantors and choir members. These and other leadership gifts are found within the membership of every parish. Those priests who possess such special gifts will share in the leadership of the liturgy when the priesthood assembles each Lord's Day.

The meaning of corporate worship is further encouragement that lay persons be given leadership roles in the celebration of the parish liturgy. Because the congregation is a sign of the household of faith and because worship is understood to be the weekly reunion of the baptized family of God, the church's rubrics expect that leadership roles will be shared:

> The liturgy is the celebration of all who gather. Together with the pastor who presides, the entire congregation is involved. It is important, therefore, that lay persons fulfill appropriate ministries within the service. (*LBW Ministers Edition*, page 25)

This rubric has become one of the liturgical hallmarks of the Lutheran church. No other denomination provides a similar rubrical insistence that lay persons occupy prominent leadership positions within the liturgy. For Lutherans, it is not enough that lay persons light the candles and read the lessons. Any part of the liturgy which does not require the leadership of an ordained minister may be led by trained lay leaders. Even in those parishes having several clergy on the staff, the use of lay liturgical leaders is expected. In those parishes, one pastor serves throughout the liturgy as the presiding minister. To maintain the integrity of the rite and to preserve the identity of the presider as a sign of Christ, the presiding minister's assignments should not be divided among the clergy present. Instead, with one pastor serving as presider, other clergy could share the tasks of announcing the day, reading the Gospel, preaching the sermon, and assisting with the distribution of the bread during Communion. The other roles assigned to assisting ministers would be fulfilled by lay leaders.

It is a high privilege to participate in the church's liturgy. Whether one is clergy or lay, there is always something astonishingly awesome about being intimately involved in the celebration of the liturgy. This is especially true during times of leadership when one handles the divine properties of Word and Sacrament and when one is being used by the Holy Spirit to tell and celebrate the

S. Anita Stauffer

mighty acts of God. It is unlike any other experience known on earth, because the church's liturgy of Word and Sacrament finds heaven and earth in intersection. It's the sovereign God holding audience for those who bear the sign of the cross, accepting their praise and receiving their prayers. Before such a Presence, "the church on earth and the hosts of heaven" assemble to unite their voices in praise and solemn delight for all that God has done and continues to do for the health and salvation of the world. In the midst of these profound sacrifices of adoration and thanksgiving, God again takes the initiative to address the people's needs, making each celebration of Word and Sacrament a new event in salvation history. With the Word that is proclaimed and with the Communion that is given, the people receive direction, encouragement, nourishment, consolation, enlightenment, forgiveness, peace, and hope. God acts for these people in this place through this liturgy, even as God acted wondrously through other events in salvation history.

Through the church's liturgy of Word and Sacrament, the promise that our Lord is with us always is again fulfilled. For this reason the celebration of such a liturgy is recognized, perceived, and celebrated as a consequential encounter with God. To participate in such an encounter is to be present where God most assuredly is, where God most assuredly speaks, and where God most assuredly acts. Liturgical leadership has the high calling to let all of that become most assuredly obvious to those who assemble before the altar of God each Lord's Day.

Future pastors spend many months in the seminary developing a style of worship leadership that is appropriate for this liturgical encounter with God. It is not enough for them to know the history of liturgy, what it means and what it promises. Seminarians also learn that good celebrations rely heavily upon the liturgical deportment, style, and attitude of the presiding minister. The way they walk in procession, how they use their voices, how they sit and stand, the gestures and ritual actions they use, the condition of their vestments, their personal hygiene, how they handle holy things, and their own involvement in the liturgical event are also given attention. A good leadership style includes a sense of reverence and awe, of hospitality and naturalness. It's a leadership style that is unique to liturgical events, and it requires time and experience to develop.

This glimpse into seminary training serves as a reminder that liturgical leadership of any kind deserves careful and reverent preparation. Those who will serve as assisting ministers should never be buttonholed or recruited in the narthex just before the service. The liturgy deserves better preparation; people deserve better treatment. Parishes are expected, therefore, to select persons whose spiritual life is apparent and to provide an effective training program for those who exercise any kind of leadership in the weekly liturgy. This includes the training of acolytes, musicians, ushers, lectors, cantors, altar guild members, choir members, and other assisting ministers. Since these are persons who have liturgical assignments, obviously they ought to receive instruction regarding the various rites and traditions of the church. With this basic instruction should come the practical descriptions and demonstrations of what is expected of them. An opportunity to rehearse their tasks again and again should be expected and provided. One need never apologize for insisting on thoroughness when preparing to lead worship.

What is hoped for in this emphasis on instruction and training is a service of worship that enables the church to tell effectively and to celebrate meaningfully the mighty acts of God. The focus and center of such a service is God in Word and Meal. It is no accident that the altar occupies the most prominent position in the worship space; the altar is a sign of the presence of God. Nor is it an accident that the art and symbols that are seen in that space, the vestments that are worn, the music that is heard—all direct our thoughts and hearts toward God. Similarly, that is also the assignment given to each person having a liturgical leadership role: to keep the attention of the congregation focused on the presence and person of God. The acolyte who scratches and yawns through the liturgy or who picks up the wrong book for the Gospel procession could avoid being such a distraction if he or she understood the meaning of worship and of liturgical leadership. So, too, the lector who confuses the word *immortal* with *immoral* or *Alpha* with *alfalfa* obscures the church's message. Such mistakes may be humorous, but they divert the attention of the people, and the testimony of God's Word is weakened.

This emphasis on training and the desirability to develop competence in leadership may offer some clues about who should be recruited for such liturgical assignments. When recruiting persons for leadership roles, parishes will want to be alert to those members who possess the gifts that such assignments require. Obviously, it is of no use to ask a monotone to serve as the cantor or a three-year-old to be the lector. There are persons, however, who have the natural or acquired skills to serve in the various roles of liturgical leadership. For example, some have the ability to serve effectively as acolytes. These persons possess the common sense and the natural talent to perform such a task with grace, ease, reverence, and competence. Such people can be found in every parish, from subteens to subcentenarians; age is not the issue any more than sex is. Ability, interest, and a desire to glorify God—these represent the most desirable traits for serving as an acolyte. Compelling a young person to serve as acolyte simply on the basis of enrollment in a confirmation class may not produce the kind of effective leadership that is needed. As St. Paul indicated, we have "gifts that differ according to the grace given to us" (Romans 12:6a). Not everyone can be an acolyte; not everyone should be asked.

Similarly, merely because someone has been elected to membership on the church council does not signify that such a person possesses the skills and gifts that make a competent Communion assistant. There are persons in every parish, however, who are willing to be trained to serve in that role. It is a rewarding task to search for such persons, inviting them to receive the necessary training, granting them an opportunity for unusual usefulness. Persons having liturgical leadership roles should be visible signs of an inclusive church: women, men, people of color, youth, older members, people who are physically impaired. Any member who can fulfill the task with competence and reverence is qualified to serve as a lay liturgical leader.

What about the use of children as assisting ministers? Since worship is a family reunion and our Lord urges us to "forbid them not," children deserve to share in the celebration of the liturgy. Depending upon their level of competence, children may also fulfill certain leadership roles. Most children enjoy the chance to sing. Since Lutherans make so much use of music in worship, there are several opportunities to use children's voices during the liturgy. For example, a children's choir could be trained to sing the bids of the *Kyrie* on occasion, or to lead the singing of the Psalm, or the appointed Verse and Offertory. Such a choir could sing a hymn in alternation with the congregation, provide an anthem, or sing with the adult choir during some choral pieces. Using Orff instruments, children can provide accompaniment for some of these selections. For some services, children can participate in the procession. For example, on the festival of the Epiphany, children could carry the figures of the magi to the creche, along with the gifts of gold, frankincense, and myrrh.

Using young children as lectors or in other such roles is not advised. Being an assisting minister requires a training and a maturity that only age and experience can provide. In most situations, only those who have reached and exceeded confirmation age should be recruited to serve as assisting ministers.

BASIC GUIDANCE

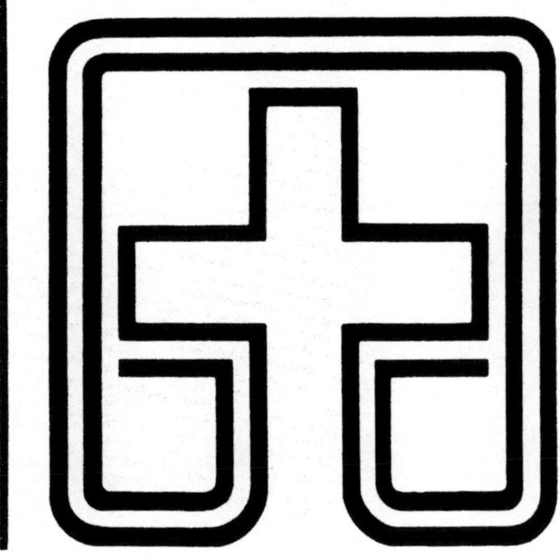

S. Anita Stauffer

This section of the handbook addresses a series of subjects that relate to the fundamentals of liturgical leadership. Tradition accounts for many practices that are continued by the church, practices which still have value to us. Such a list of traditions includes the use of the church year calendar and lectionary, colors of the church year, candles and flowers, pulpits, organs, cross and crucifix, bells, vestments, kneeling, bowing the head and folding one's hands for prayer, and stained glass windows. Such a list of traditions could go on and on. In fact, the liturgy itself has been shaped through the ages by centuries of accumulated learnings as the church has sought to offer worthy worship to God the Creator, Redeemer, and Sanctifier. Wisdom encourages today's church to continue to explore the treasury of richness and inspiration that tradition provides.

During the days of the Reformation, Lutherans had opportunity to test this principle of tradition. Some emerging denominations at that time felt constrained to discard any and all liturgical practices which seemed not to be commanded by Holy Scripture. In some places, this decision prompted their members to break all stained glass windows, to smash pipe organs, to burn vestments, to discard altars, and to replace the historic liturgy with an improvised order of service.

Lutherans took a position that was in sharp contrast to that. Those traditions which were not in conflict with the Gospel of grace were kept intact. After all, Lutheranism saw itself not as a new denomination, but as a reforming movement within the established church. Such traditions as the use of crucifixes, the sign of the cross, incense, the church year, bells, elevation of the Host in Communion, vestments, and the historic Mass itself were not abolished but cherished and continued:

> . . . we do not abolish the Mass but religiously keep and defend it. In our churches Mass is celebrated every Sunday and on other festivals, when the sacrament is offered to those who wish for it after they have been examined and absolved. We keep traditional liturgical forms, such as the order of the lessons, prayers, vestments, etc. *(Apology of the Augsburg Confession*, Article XXIV)

Such a conscious decision to retain such traditions represents a liturgical hallmark of Lutheranism.

Most liturgical practices have been formed by the liturgical event itself, because of the awareness that the celebration of the liturgy places us in the holy presence of the Most High God. That awareness makes a significant contribution to the way and the manner we conduct ourselves; it also determines what is said and sung in such a place for such an event. It is for this reason that a discussion of tradition begins with a reference to reverence.

REVERENCE

Reverence is primarily an attitude, an awesome reaction to an awesome Reality. Reverence is usually reserved for those situations when God is encountered, when God's presence is sensed, when God's nearness is perceived. It is the sort of quiet emotion that seems to cradle the heart during times of Absolution and Communion. Reverence is more than a feeling, more than a sensation. It is a form of divine domination, when the heart makes more sense than the head and we are conscious of a loving Reality that is beyond any human measurement.

Reverence cannot be manufactured, nor can it be commanded rubrically. However, worship leaders are expected to do their tasks in ways which foster reverence and devotion. That is not an attempt to create an artificial or counterfeit mood among the worshipers. Rather, it is to exercise a stewardship of the event through words and actions, deportment and demeanor, so that everyone can detect the unique and divine character of this encounter with God. The liturgy is, after all, an involvement in a mystery. Through Word and Sacrament God is present and is in action in this place, in this time, and with these people. It is difficult to find a more accurate word than reverence when attempting to describe the appropriate attitude and actions for worshipers and for worship leaders.

For the worship leader, reverence begins during service preparation time as each role is carefully rehearsed, as needed items are put in place, as vestments are put on, and as the procession is formed. Through it all, each leader is keenly sensitive to what is about to happen: the church is about to be engaged in an event which brings the saints of heaven and earth together in holy assembly before the throne of God. This is far more significant than providing leadership for a religious program or conducting a study class or merely leading an order of service. The church's holy liturgy is about to be celebrated, reverently recalling salvation history, reverently offering the sacrifice of adoration to God, and reverently receiving those gifts of grace that transform and sustain the people of God.

For the worship leader, this sense of mystery and encounter with the holy persists as the procession enters, as the Word of God is proclaimed, as the prayers are offered, and as the Peace is shared. This sense of mystery and expectation acquires a new intensity as the holy Meal is readied and blessed and received. It persists until, finally, the priesthood shouts "Thanks be to God!" and returns to the world which waits for that Word which only Christians can share.

HOSPITALITY

To express reverence through the liturgical event is the worship leader's response to a divine Reality. There is another reality in this event which the worship leader also needs to note. It's the human reality, the awareness that it is people who worship. The convocation of priests is also an assembly of human beings. Despite the fact that they are the baptized priests of God, some of them probably did not feel very much like attending worship. Some may be very tired, worn out after a demanding week. Some may be filled with dread or fear or guilt. Some of those present may be locked in sorrow. Some who are present may be strangers to the Gospel.

Because of this human reality and because we recognize that worship is the reunion of a very human family, reverence has a companion word for those who serve as worship leaders—*hospitality*. This is the word which describes an appropriate leadership style for those who serve as ushers, acolytes, musicians, greeters, assisting ministers, and presiding minister. It's a leadership style that demonstrates openness and acceptance and friendship. It communicates cordiality and graciousness and amiability. Hospitality prevents reverence from becoming mere ritualism. Reverence prevents hospitality from becoming boorish.

The desire to give expression to hospitality accounts for many of the ritual actions that are a part of the liturgical celebration. The presiding minister's gesture of extending open arms and hands to the congregation during the Apostolic Greeting is a sign of liturgical hospitality. It's a way of embracing everyone present, drawing them all into the action of worship. Similar gestures of hospitality are repeated during the Salutation and the Peace. This desire to be hospitable is one reason why the church recommends that the altar be freestanding. This permits the presiding and assisting ministers to face the congregation during the Great Thanksgiving, and it enables the congregation to have a more intimate involvement with the preparation and blessing of the Eucharistic Meal.

Attitudes and actions of hospitality are also expected from the assisting minister. Among other things, this means serving before the people in a way that suggests delight at being involved in this liturgical event. This does not mean the flashing of wide grins throughout the service. It simply requires giving expression to graciousness and warmth without jeopardizing reverence.

Assisting ministers are liturgically hospitable when they look directly at the congregation as the readings are announced, when they open and raise their arms during the prayers they offer, when they look at each communicant as they offer the cup, and when they look directly at the people during the words of dismissal: "Go in peace. Serve the Lord." Obviously, these are looks of cordiality and of reverent hospitality.

VESTMENTS

Vestments represent an important part of Lutheranism's liturgical tradition. Vestments are those special items of clothing worn by worship leaders, both clergy and lay persons. In one sense, such liturgical clothing may be regarded as uniforms, in the sense of wearing that which is appropriate for this unusual event. It's a tradition that has enjoyed a long history in the church, in use as early as the fourth century. Before that time, worship leaders wore their usual, everyday clothing for the liturgy; the only requirement was that their clothing had to be clean. But then fashions began to change. The long, ankle-length robes that had been worn for centuries were being replaced by very short tunics. Objections were raised against clergy wearing such clothing for the liturgy, causing the church to express a preference for those items that had been common during the times of the apostles. This decision established a visible linkage to

S. Anita Stauffer

the days when the church was founded, and it erased the need to determine proper liturgical clothing every time fashions changed.

Even so, there has been an evolution of liturgical vesture since those early centuries. For example, surplices and albs can be worn by all worship leaders, but only those who are ordained wear the stole and chasuble. In addition, not all vestments are worn for all services; what is worn is determined by the kind of service being celebrated.

One of the compelling reasons for continuing the tradition of wearing vestments is to keep our attention focused on what the liturgy is all about. This is the same reason we use crosses, paraments, banners, and art glass windows. Each of these discourages our minds from wandering from that which is central—the celebration of the Gospel. Wearing vestments also reminds worship leaders what their role and task should be. In addition, vestments equalize those who wear them; the service does not become an occasion for the parish fashion plates to parade their recent acquisitions.

Our tradition provides several options when selecting vestments for the celebration of the Holy Communion. Vestments for the assisting ministers are selected on the basis of what is worn by the presiding minister. Traditionally, pectoral crosses are worn only by bishops.

In most parishes, the presiding minister wears an alb, cincture, and stole for the Holy Communion liturgy. The *alb* is a full-length white vestment, regarded as the basic eucharistic vestment. It is usually worn with a *cincture*, a long white rope tied around the waist. The *stole* is a scarf-like vestment worn over the shoulders by clergy as a sign of their ordination to the ministry of Word and Sacrament. Stoles are worn in the colors of the church year. If the stole is crossed over the breast of the wearer, its ends are laced through the cincture to keep the stole in place. Often the presiding minister wears a chasuble over the alb, cincture, and stole. The *chasuble*, shaped very much like a poncho, is made in the colors of the church year. It is the principal eucharistic vestment and is worn only by the ordained presiding minister and only for the Holy Communion. When the presiding minister wears an alb, with or without chasuble, it is appropriate for the assisting ministers to wear albs and cinctures. Lay assisting ministers never wear stoles or chasubles.

As an alternative to the alb, sometimes the presiding minister wears a cassock, surplice, and stole, although the cassock and surplice are traditionally limited to non-eucharistic services (such as Morning and Evening Prayer, Compline, The Litany, or the Service of the Word). The *cassock* is a long, ankle-length vestment with narrow sleeves. A black vestment, the cassock has traditionally served as the basic, everyday work clothes of the clergy. The *surplice* is a long white vestment with long and rather full sleeves. The surplice evolved from the alb, though no cincture is worn with it. When the surplice is worn, it is always worn over a cassock. When the presiding minister wears cassock and surplice, it is appropriate for the assisting ministers to wear cassocks and cottas or surplices. The *cotta* is a full, white vestment which is similar to the surplice, except that it is cut shorter.

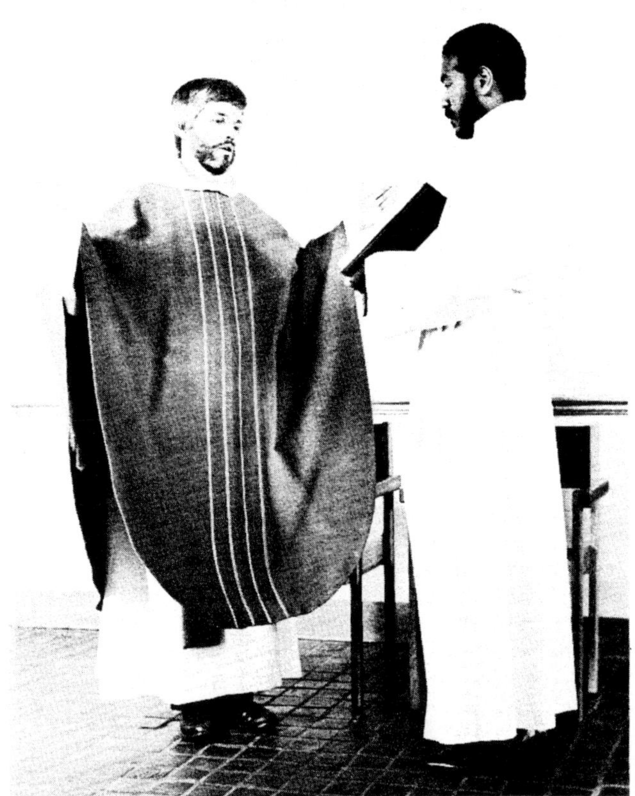
Stan Sadowski

For some festival services, the cope may be worn as a procession vestment. The *cope* is a rather full cape, made in the colors of the church year. It may also be worn to lead some services that do not include the celebration of the Holy Communion (Morning Prayer, Evening Prayer). However, it is not a vestment for clergy only. If a lay person is the principal minister for a prayer service, such as Morning or Evening Prayer, that person may be vested in a cope.

Vestments should not be confused with robes. A robe is a garment useful to bathers. It is also a word used to describe academic garb. However, when the church makes reference to the liturgical clothing worn by acolytes, choir members, musicians, presiding minister, and assisting ministers, the word is *vestments*. Lutherans do not have "robing rooms" in their churches, only vesting rooms.

When selecting vestments for acolytes, musicians, choir, confirmation class, clergy, and lay ministers, those that are similar to judicial and academic robes ought to be avoided. Such robes suggest that worship is only a teaching event presided over by professors, or some kind of a trial presided over by a judge. Using liturgical vestments enables the assembly to perceive the nature, character, and uniqueness of the worship service.

BEFORE THE SERVICE

As worship leaders gather before the service to put on their vestments, for them the liturgy has begun. It ought to

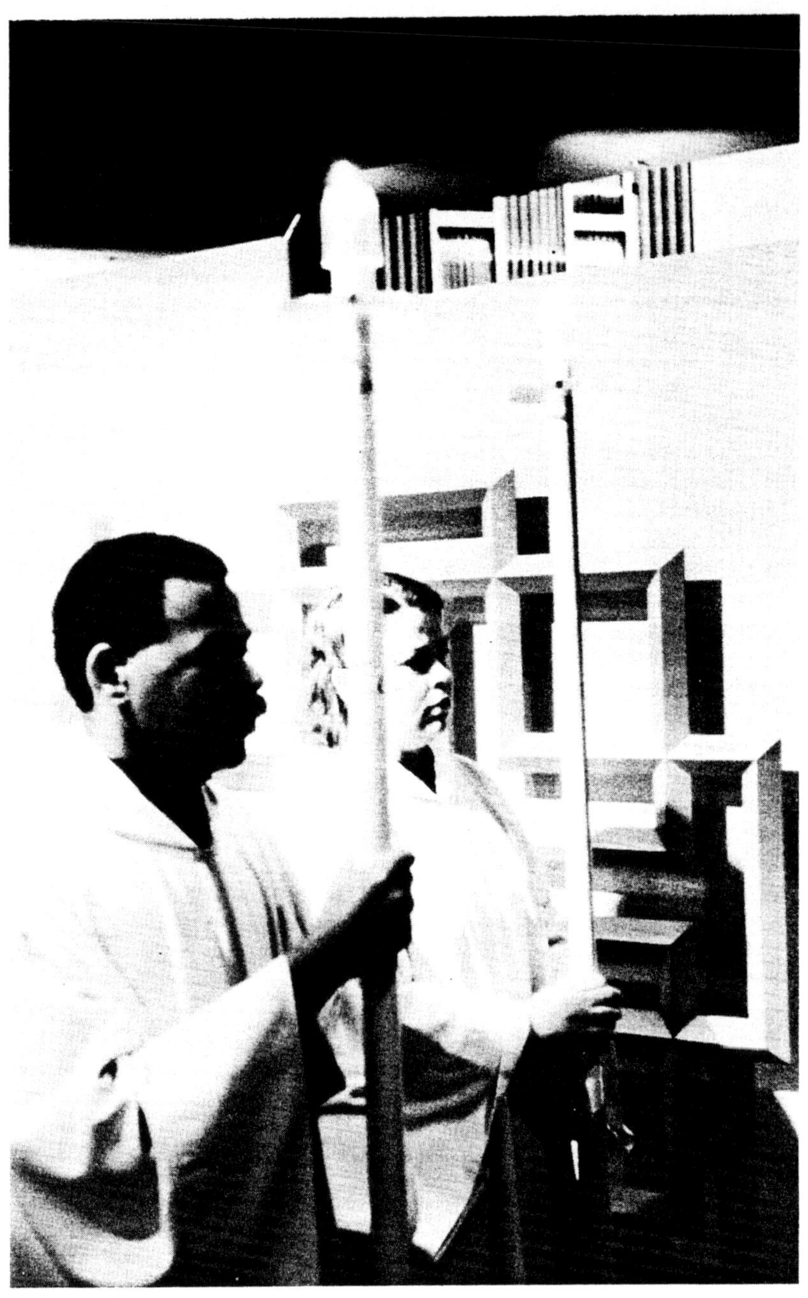

Ralph R. Van Loon

be a quiet time, a time to prepare one's heart and mind for the holy tasks that await. It is a time to make the transition from being caught up in the things of this world to that moment when the procession signals entry into the throne room of God. Obviously, vesting time is not a time for levity or idle conversation, nor for getting one last sip of coffee. Instead, hands are washed, hair is combed, visible jewelry is removed, books are marked, and last-minute instructions are given. Then clean vestments are taken from their storage place and are put on carefully. A full-length mirror can assure that the vestment has been properly buttoned and tied and that it hangs neatly. Each assists the other in this process, giving special attention to the younger persons who are vesting.

When all are vested and all have in hand whatever is to be carried in procession, a sacristy prayer such as the following is offered:

Almighty God, you pour out on all who desire it the spirit of grace and supplication. Deliver us, as we come into your presence, from cold hearts and wandering thoughts, that with steady minds and burning zeal we may worship you in spirit and in truth; through your Son, Jesus Christ our Lord. Amen (LBW, page 47)

Bless us, O God, with a reverent sense of your presence, that we may be at peace and may worship you with all our mind and spirit; through Jesus Christ our Lord. Amen (LBW, page 47)

O Jesus, our great high priest, be present with us as you were present with your disciples and make yourself known to us in the breaking of bread. (LBW, page 47)

PROCESSIONS

Depending upon the kind of service being celebrated, processions can be quite simple or quite elaborate. A simple procession can include as few as two persons, whereas a festival procession could consist of several. Ordinarily, a procession of some kind will be used at every celebration of the Holy Communion; it is a sign of our Lord's entry into the midst of his assembled priesthood. The presiding minister, whom the church has ordained to serve in the stead of Christ during the liturgy, provides such a sign and walks last in the procession. Others in the procession are understood to be in the retinue of our Lord; they also enter in procession according to their assignment in the liturgy. Because the procession, simple or elaborate, marks the entrance of our Lord, the congregation always stands to welcome the church's High Priest. If a processional cross is carried in, it is customary for the congregation to turn toward it, each head bowing as the cross passes, as a sign of respect for this emblem of our redemption.

The order of procession for a nonfestival celebration would be:

Processional cross, flanked by processional torches

Assisting minister, carrying the *LBW Ministers Edition*

Assisting minister, carrying the Bible or lectionary

Presiding minister

Note that the choir is not included in this order of procession. It is preferred that the choir will have entered in advance of the procession, perhaps during a prelude. This enables the choir to be in place during the Brief Order for Confession and Forgiveness and to support the congregation during the Entrance Hymn. If it is necessary for the choir to enter via the center aisle of the nave, it is suggested that the choir make its entrance silently, walking in pairs, each bowing the head toward the altar before turning to be seated.

Also note in the above order of procession that the ministers walk in single file. This gives greater prominence to the items being carried for use during the celebration of the liturgy.

The order of procession for a festival celebration would be:

Processional cross, flanked by processional torches

Bannerbearer, carrying seasonal banner

Bookbearer, carrying the Bible or lectionary

Assisting minister (lector)

Assisting minister (lector, intercessor)

Assisting minister (principal), carrying the *LBW Ministers Edition*

Preacher

Presiding minister

If the choir is to be included in the procession for festivals, it would be placed just before the seasonal banner.

On those rare occasions when a high festival celebration is desired to mark a particularly significant event, the following order of procession may be used:

Thurifer, with burning censer

Acolyte, with incense boat

Crucifer, carrying processional cross

Torchbearers, carrying lighted processional candles

Bannerbearer, carrying seasonal banner

Bookbearer, carrying Bible or lectionary

Preacher

Master of ceremonies

Presiding minister, wearing cope, flanked by assisting ministers serving as subdeacon and deacon

The processional route for such a festival service would be from the sacristy to the rear of the church (by way of the middle aisle, if the sacristy is in the front of the nave), then to the front of the church by way of the north (Gospel) aisle, proceeding across the front of the nave to the rear of the church via the south (Epistle) aisle, returning to the altar via the center aisle. During this procession, an appropriate litany, psalm, or hymn may be sung. When the procession concludes at the altar, the cope is removed from the presiding minister and exchanged for the chasuble. If the preacher is vested in a cope, it is worn until the time of the sermon.

At any service in which there is to be a procession out, the order of procession remains the same.

An entrance procession is more than a matter of moving people from one place to another. It is a liturgical act, signaling the approach and entry of our Lord into the midst of his baptized household of believers. Again he comes to his people with Word and Sacrament to minister, to encourage, to forgive, and to give hope. Such a procession expects much from those who are privileged to be a part of our Lord's retinue: they are to announce his coming and to herald his approach. This suggests that procession participants fulfill their assignment with reverence, making it obvious that each knows the signficance of this liturgical action.

At a signal provided by the presiding minister, the crucifer leads the procession into the gathered assembly. The crucifer (or thurifer) holds the processional cross straight and upright, using both hands to keep the cross stabilized and to allow for varying ceiling heights. Two torchbearers accompany the crucifer, holding the processional torches straight and upright to prevent melted wax from spilling. The crucifer and torchbearers set the pace of the procession. Therefore, it is necessary that these persons be carefully rehearsed, since walking too fast or too slowly creates problems for those at the end of the procession. Walking naturally with good posture and maintaining a distance of about two yards between each unit help to produce an orderly and effective procession.

Those in the procession who have items to carry for the service should hold them as objects for the congregation to see. The processional cross should be held aloft for all to see the majesty of our primary symbol. The flames of the processional torches ought to be above the heads of the torchbearers, who have been trained to maintain stability and safety. A banner used in procession also needs to be held high for all to see its symbols.

Books to be used during the service, the Bible (or lectionary) and the *LBW Ministers Edition*, are often carried in procession. Each may be regarded as another form of banner, carried for all to see. Such processional books require the use of both hands; the book's spine is usually in the left hand. When carried during a procession, the book should be held at least at shoulder height. Also, one would not carry modestly proportioned or modestly bound books for such a procession; small and paperback editions cannot convey the importance we attach to the church's books.

Persons in the procession who have nothing to carry walk with their hands folded at the waist. This is a good procedure to follow at all times during the service, whether in procession or standing or moving about the chancel. Hands may be folded in one of two ways: first, there is the ancient style referred to as "a temple," in which the open hands are brought together with thumbs crossed and fingers pointed upward at an angle; second, there is the more familiar style of clasping the hands together with the fingers of both hands intertwined. Whichever style is used, the hands are always joined and held at the waist.

POSTURES

Tradition also offers counsel regarding other postures for worship leaders during the liturgical celebration. While stiffness and stuffiness should be avoided, conducting oneself with a sense of reverence is always appropriate for those who help the congregation discover the meaning of this encounter with God. A worship leader who is slouchy, slovenly, or sloppy is an impediment to the event. Such leaders prevent worshipers from gaining a glimpse of the glory of God; they whisk away any suggestion of holy mystery; and they divert attention from God to themselves. What is needed for worship leadership are persons who love God, who love the worship of God, and who want, above all, to enable other worshipers to behold the presence and glory of God. One does not have to assume a different personality to be such a leader. Being aware of the radical significance of this encounter with God and letting that awareness find expression in the way leadership is exercised—that is what is useful to the liturgy and to those who have come to worship. Such an awareness prompts both reverence and hospitality.

Joseph McGinty

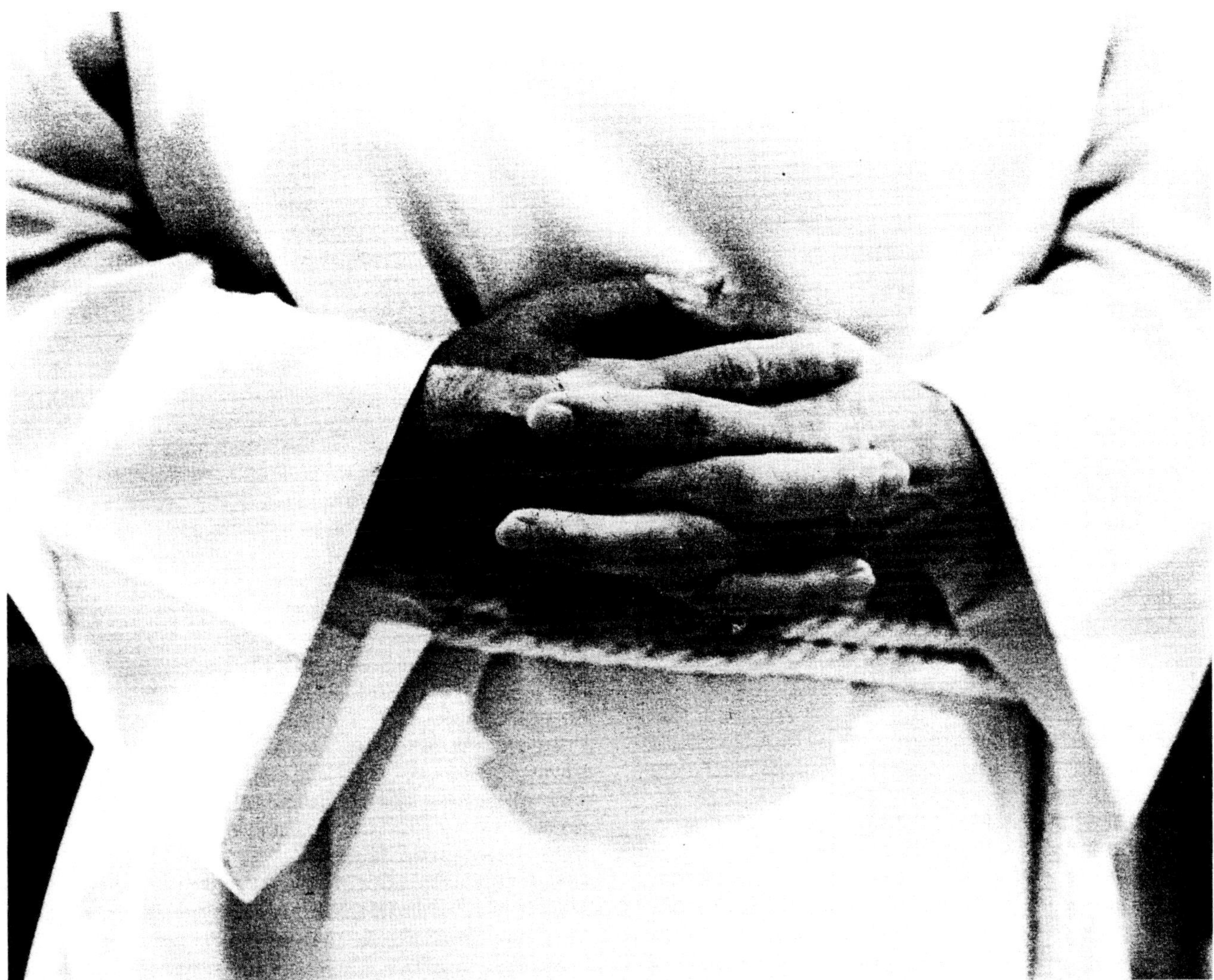

S. Anita Stauffer

It is very common to stand for many parts of the liturgy. For Christians, this is a sign of resurrection and an appropriate posture for offering praise. As a symbol of the resurrection, worship leaders are provided with a clue as to how they ought to stand. Whether the leader is standing because the congregation is expected to do so or because a particular assignment of leadership is being addressed, the posture is the same—erect with both feet flat on the floor and hands folded at the waist unless holding a book or bulletin.

A similar kind of erectness is expected of worship leaders during those parts of the service when they are seated. Worship leaders should remember that, even when they sit, they continue to be leaders. They continue to be visible to other worshipers; they continue to be perceived as model worshipers. Therefore, worship leaders will be very conscious of the image and example they are projecting even while they are seated. They will sit erectly. They will give full attention to what is being read or sung or done or preached. During the reading of the lessons, worship leaders will keep their eyes on the lector and their ears open to the reading. Their heads will not be buried in the bulletin; they will not be whispering with persons seated nearby; and they will not be looking into the congregation. They will always be attentive and alert and interested in what is being said, sung, read, or done. Such attention will be obvious when each worship leader is seated erectly with hands folded comfortably on the lap. Arms should not be thrown over the back of the chair, and legs should not be crossed or stuck straight out in front. Worship leaders, when seated, will demonstrate that they continue to fulfill their leadership role.

Kneeling is another posture used in worship. It happens during confession, and in many places it is customary to kneel to receive Communion. Especially for those times when penitence and humility are being expressed, it is appropriate to kneel. Again, an erect posture is called for.

RITUAL ACTIONS

For worshipers and worship leaders, the liturgy provides a series of ritual actions which enable a communication and celebration more profound than words. These actions include making the sign of the cross, bowing, and exchanging the sign of Peace. Ritual actions become a part of the Christian experience very early in life. Such ritual actions are taught to children because they are useful and enriching traditions. Early in life, our parents show us how to bow our heads, close our eyes, and fold our hands for prayer. These are ritual actions, and they are firmly implanted within us.

As Lutherans, there are some additional ritual actions that we treasure, recognizing that they are inextricably bound to our liturgical life. At Baptism, when through water and the Spirit we are made members of God's redeemed family, the pastor traces the sign of the cross upon us. That is our mark of membership in the priesthood of all believers. It is God's way of marking each of us forever as God's own child. At Baptism, the sign of the cross is traced upon us, giving us a new identity and a new destiny as those who are now joined to the death and resurrection of our Lord.

Every day we recall that unique identity, as instructed by Martin Luther, by tracing the sign of the cross. It is not surprising that the liturgy of the baptized includes such a ritual action, encouraging all present to recall who they are and to what they have been called. For Christians it is an action that comes so naturally; it seems to require only a minimum of instruction: the right hand is raised to touch one's forehead, then lowered to the breast, then to touch the left shoulder and then the right shoulder, and finally back to the center of the chest. For people of the cross, making the sign of the cross is as comfortable and natural as breathing.

The church's liturgy also provides for the exchange of the sign of Peace. From the earliest moment of our history, Christians have found this to be a profoundly meaningful ritual action. As they speak the words of the Peace of the Lord and accompany those words with an embrace or a handshake, Christians are communicating a profound truth. It is a sign of our unity through Holy Baptism—a convincing and a public demonstration that through our reconciliation with God, we are also reconciled to one another; that we are bound together in one holy fellowship; and that we should care deeply about one another.

The exchange of the Peace is a sacred and significant moment in the church's liturgy. It is not a time for idle chatter or the exchange of pleasantries; it's the time to recall and to celebrate the "peace of God, which passes all understanding" (Philippians 4:7). It's a time to reach out to other worshipers—to family and to strangers, to friends as well as to those with whom we may have had a conflict—sharing that which has been shared with us, the Peace of the Lord.

As the one who serves the worshiping assembly as a sign of Christ, the presiding minister initiates the Peace by speaking to all the words of Peace. The presiding minister then exchanges the Peace with the assisting ministers; together they exchange that sign with other worship leaders as worshipers embrace one another. All the worship leaders share in that exchange.

Because they recognize the import and meaning of this ritual action, worship leaders will make a full investment in its implementation. Without timidity or self-consciousness, and without buffoonery or boisterousness, worship leaders will engage in the Peace with sensitivity, reverence, hospitality, and cordiality.

Bowing is another ritual action that occupies a firm position in our liturgical tradition. A distinction is usually made between a bow, which is simply a nod of the head, and a profound bow, which is bowing from the waist. Liturgically, bowing is a sign of respect, of humility, and of devotion. It's what we do during a prayer, when we are

John Jorgenson

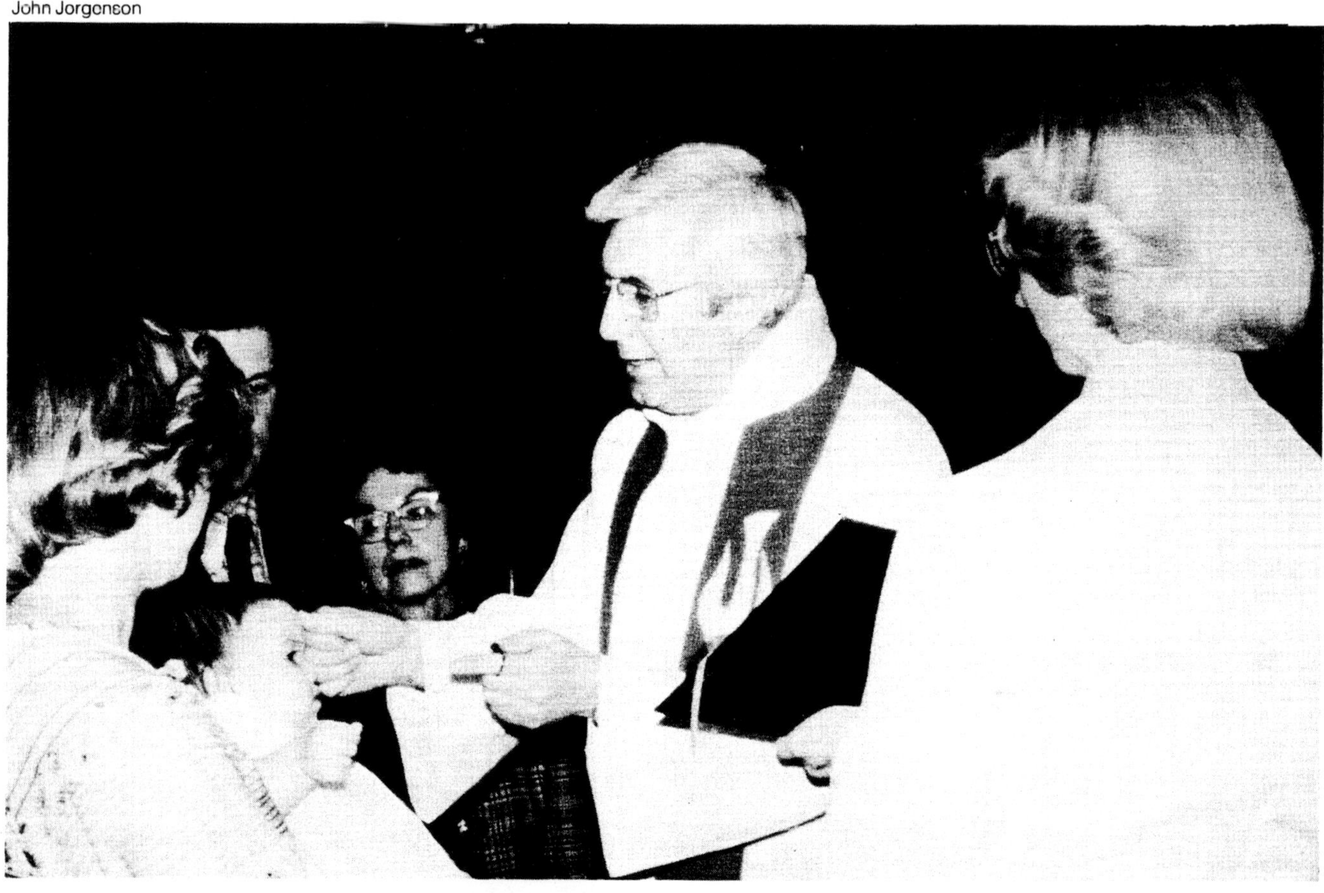

being absolved, and when we receive a blessing. A bowed head during those moments indicates involvement and receptivity and reverence. Bowing the head when the processional cross passes, when we approach the altar, and when we pass in front of the altar becomes a public witness to the fact that we recognize and respect the Reality who stands behind those basic symbols of our faith. It's exercising a common courtesy toward an uncommon actuality.

A posture of prayer used by worship leaders is referred to as the *orans*. This is a Latin word for prayer and is used to describe a ritual action which can claim a very long history. It's one of those liturgical traditions of the Old Testament that Christians continued to use in their own worship (cf. Psalm 63:4, 1 Timothy 2:8). They did so because the orans posture of prayer expresses in a unique way the nature of corporate supplication; that is, the open and raised arms of the one praying suggest that our prayers are ascending to the throne of God and are being offered for the entire assembly. As such, the orans posture is in sharp contrast to the practice of clasping one's hands at the waist and bowing the head; this is, of course, a perfectly proper way to pray. However, when prayers are being offered by a liturgical leader on behalf of those gathered, then a posture which seems to embrace all worshipers present is preferred.

The orans posture for prayer is easily learned. As is true for all ritual actions, it should be done with grace and with a sense of naturalness. Folded hands at the waist are separated and slowly swoop upward and extend outward until the hands are at about eye level. The hands are slightly cupped; fingers are not separated. Perhaps it is helpful to understand that the orans finds the minister holding the chalice of our corporate petitions to the lips of God.

Because worship leaders have high visibility throughout the service, their own liturgical conduct and their own use of ritual actions and postures always help shape the liturgical attitudes and conduct of the worshiping congregation. Leadership plays a heavy role in establishing the mood and character of the event. If the leadership knows that the celebration of the liturgy is an event of great and holy consequence and gives full and reverent expression to that awareness, the people will quickly perceive that they are here involved in a divine dynamic which is supremely relevant for the church and for the world. Sunday morning with Word and Sacrament is of high importance to God and to God's people; through their words and through their actions, worship leaders demonstrate their recognition of this fact. Worship leaders will rejoice that they have this opportunity for unusual usefulness.

Stan Sadowski

LEADING THE LITURGY

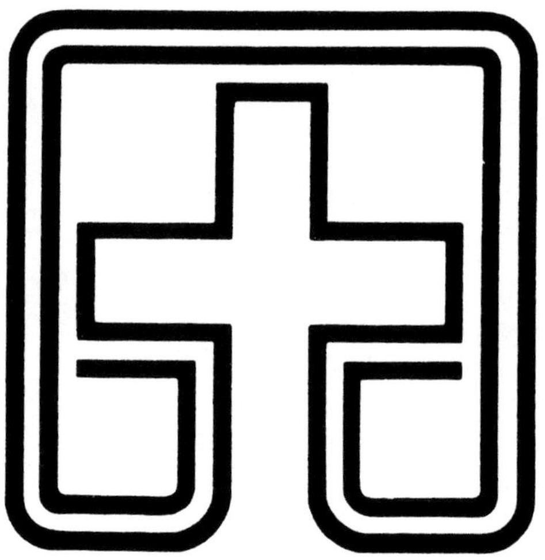

This section focuses particularly on those tasks which the rubrics assign to assisting ministers. As this section is reviewed, it will be helpful to have at hand a copy of the *Lutheran Book of Worship* and the *LBW Ministers Desk Edition*, referring to those pages which contain the service of Holy Communion.

The Holy Communion liturgy has several sections. Each section relates to the others; all the parts are interlocking.

Where the presiding and assisting ministers stand for each part of the service is important. In fact, this matter needs to be thought through carefully for each part of the liturgy. Not too many years ago, it was generally assumed that the entire liturgy would be led from the altar. The only exception was the sermon, for which the pastor usually moved to the pulpit. The LBW encourages us to recognize that each part of the service has its own character, its own distinctive role in the holy drama of the liturgy. These distinctive roles are more easily detected when the congregation can focus on a variety of liturgical centers within the church.

This accounts for the counsel that the baptismal font be large, amply proportioned, and prominently situated. The size and location of the font can make a strong statement about the importance of Holy Baptism; it also permits the baptistery to have liturgical usages beyond that of Baptism itself. For instance, the font can be the liturgical center for the Brief Order for Confession and Forgiveness. As the congregation gives attention to the font for this brief preparatory rite, the linkages of Baptism with repentance and forgiveness become more obvious.

The first section of the liturgy itself is the entrance rite—the Entrance Hymn (sung during the entrance procession), the Apostolic Greeting, the Kyrie and/or the Hymn of the Day, and the Salutation and Prayer of the Day. The entrance rite not only draws all the people together into one single household of worshipers; it also points to the characteristics and focus of the day's celebration. The liturgical center for the Apostolic Greeting through the Prayer of the Day could be the sedilia where the presiding and assisting ministers stand, perhaps facing toward the congregation. An alternate location would be on the nave level at the front of the center aisle.

The second section of the service is known as the liturgy of the Word; it takes us from the First Lesson through the intercessory Prayers. This section of the service is based on the liturgy used in synagogues during the time of the apostles, and it was well known to early Christians. The liturgy of the Word gives attention to the proclamation of God's Word especially through readings from the Bible and a sermon based on those readings. This part of the service centers around the place of the Word—that place where God's holy Word is read and preached. At those services where a Gospel procession is included and the Holy Gospel is read in the midst of the congregation, an additional liturgical center is realized. The intercessory Prayers may be led from the sedilia.

The third section of the service is known as the Thanksgiving, or the liturgy of the Meal, or the Eucharist, or the Lord's Supper. This climactic part of the service is based on the rite instituted by Jesus the night he was betrayed. It begins with the exchange of the Peace; includes our offering of gifts of bread and wine and money; engages us in a Preface Dialog; sets apart bread and wine as the Body and Blood of Christ as it remembers salvation history and invokes the action of the Holy Spirit; draws us to share in that Meal of grace; and sends us out to do priesthood in the world. This third section of the service has its own unique focus—the altar. In every Lutheran church the altar occupies the most prominent position in the worship space. It is the Table of the Lord. It links us to the Upper Room, where our Lord instituted that holy Meal which sustains us as members of the household of faith. Therefore, the rubrics encourage us to delay using the altar as a place of liturgical action until the other parts of the service have been completed. Following The Prayers and the exchange of the Peace, everyone's attention shifts to the altar where preparations are made for the Lord's Supper of life and salvation.

One of the roles assigned to the assisting minister is to serve as a kind of human missal stand, holding the *LBW Ministers Edition* for the presiding minister and turning pages as necessary. This leaves the presiding minister free and unencumbered so that the expected ritual actions can be made fully and without restraint. It takes some practice to find a comfortable way to hold this large book and to hold it at the right angle for easy use by the presider. While a smaller version, the *LBW Ministers Desk Edition*, has been printed for use during study, it is not intended for use in corporate worship. The large green-covered *LBW Ministers Edition* has the size and appearance which are appropriate for use in the celebration of the liturgy.

It will be useful for the assisting minister to understand how to find the appropriate page in the *LBW Ministers Edition* as the service proceeds. Obviously, the book ribbons are used for this purpose, though it is not a matter of memorizing which color is associated with which page. Rather, it's placing the ribbons in order over the right margin of the page, knowing that the ribbon at the top marks the next page needed. Consider the following procedure: Before the service begins, pull all the ribbons free. If the Brief Order for Confession and Forgiveness is to be used this day, open the *LBW Ministers Edition* to that page. Place a ribbon at that page, letting it hang over the right margin. Next, on the page containing the Apostolic Greeting, place another ribbon over the right margin of the page, setting it just below the first ribbon. The third ribbon would be placed on the page containing the Prayer of the Day. Again, this ribbon would be set just below the previously set ribbon. Continue this same procedure until all the needed pages are marked; ribbons not needed may be inserted in the rear of the book. Then, as the service proceeds, the ribbon is moved from its position on the right margin to the center fold when that page has been used and will not be referred to again at that service. Using this system, the assisting minister always knows that it is the topmost ribbon hanging from the right edge of the book that locates the page that is needed next. The principal assisting minister should check the book prior to each service to be sure the ribbons are properly placed.

S. Anita Stauffer

BRIEF ORDER FOR CONFESSION AND FORGIVENESS

The leadership for this preparatory rite is assigned to that ordained pastor whom the liturgy refers to as the presiding minister. The presiding minister may elect to stand before the congregation to lead this rite, though the baptismal font, whether located near the front of the church or near the narthex, is prehaps a more appropriate location for the Confession. In that case, an assisting minister may be asked to accompany the presiding minister to the font and to hold open the *LBW Ministers Edition* to facilitate the action of the rite. For example, the presiding minister may dip his or her hand into water of the font just prior to the trinitarian invocation while the sign of the cross is traced. Having the assisting minister hold the book also frees the presiding minister to raise his or her hands in prayer and to trace the sign of the cross over the congregation as the Absolution is given.

THE PROCESSION AND ENTRANCE HYMN

Following the Brief Order for Confession and Forgiveness, the procession is formed. It enters the nave at a signal provided by the presiding minister, walking naturally and at the pace set by the crucifer and the torchbearers. When carrying the processional cross, the crucifer does not bow because the cross is the church's primary emblem. Since processional torches accompany, mark, and illuminate the cross, neither do torchbearers bow when they approach the altar. It is customary for the crucifer and torchbearers to lead the procession into the nave and to turn and face the congregation when they near the altar. As the other procession participants approach the front of the church, each bows toward the cross before going to his or her assigned place. The crucifer and torchbearers remain facing the congregation until the presiding minister has bowed toward the cross. That bow becomes the signal for the crucifer and torchbearers to place the cross and torches in their stands and to go to their assigned places. By this time, each banner carried in the procession also has been placed in its stand and the Bible or lectionary has been set in its place and opened to the First Lesson. When the Entrance Hymn concludes, all give full attention to the presiding minister who, in Christ's stead, gives the Apostolic Greeting to all present.

KYRIE

The bids of the Kyrie are assigned to an assisting minister. The Kyrie bids and responses are traditionally sung. If the assisting minister who serves most immediately with the presiding minister is not a singer, the bids may be sung by a cantor or by the choir or a section of the choir.

Liturgical singing is usually referred to as chanting. For most people it is easier to chant than to sing, for chanting is simply another form of speaking—it is speaking musically. One of the reasons Lutherans love to chant is not just because we have a great musical tradition, but also because chanting gives a greater intensity to what is being communicated. Singing the Kyrie bids as a vocal solo makes the assignment more difficult than it needs to be, and that's not chanting. These are not arias from a cantata or an opera and should not be sung as though they were. Chanting, or liturgical singing, is simply giving the speaking voice a musical quality. Chanting a liturgical text brings enrichment to the words, captures the ears of the people, and enhances the entire event.

Like learning to read well, it requires practice and more practice to learn how to be a good chanter. It is through practice and experience that one gains the self-confidence to be a competent assisting minister. The parish organist or music director, because of a high commitment to the important role of music in worship, will be able to provide instruction in chanting.

Since the Kyrie is sometimes omitted from the liturgy for some services, the assisting minister needs to be alert to whether or not it is to be included on a given day.

HYMN OF PRAISE

As is true for the Kyrie, the Hymn of Praise is sometimes omitted from the liturgy. The Hymn of Praise is always omitted during the seasons of Advent and Lent. The LBW provides a choice of hymns to be sung for this part of the service: "Glory to God" and "Worthy Is Christ." The season of the church year determines which is to be sung—"Worthy Is Christ" is used on the Sundays of Easter, All Saints', and Christ the King; and "Glory to God" is sung on other Sundays and festivals—although "Worthy Is Christ" should not be used when the Eucharist feast is not celebrated. An assisting minister usually serves as cantor in leading the Hymn of Praise. Like the Kyrie, the Hymn of Praise should also be carefully rehearsed.

SALUTATION AND PRAYER OF THE DAY

The Salutation and Prayer of the Day are assigned to the presiding minister. The liturgy recognizes these as "presidential" elements; the assisting minister does not ever lead this section of the liturgy, nor should the congregation pray the Prayer of the Day in unison.

The Prayer of the Day marks the conclusion of the entrance rite and the beginning of the liturgy of the Word. This prayer is never omitted from any celebration of the Holy Communion. Following this prayer, the presiding minister is seated and the assisting minister who is to read the First Lesson goes to the place of the Word.

THE FIRST LESSON

The assisting minister who reads the First and Second Lessons has the title of lector. As lector, the assisting minister is charged with one of the most important assignments of the liturgy: the proclamation of the Word of God. With such an assignment the lector becomes an agent of the Holy Spirit and an administrator of the grace of God. This is no minor role in the liturgy; to hear God's Word is one of the major reasons for doing liturgy. Without it, the liturgy doesn't happen. Without it, the people would be deprived of the counsel and consolation they all need. When the lector stands before the worshiping assembly to speak the words of Holy Scripture, God's voice is being heard and God's will is being revealed. These are the words of eternal life, and it is the lector's high calling to deliver such words to the gathered assembly.

How the lector discharges this high calling is a witness to what the church thinks about God's Word. If a lector reads thoughtlessly, carelessly, irreverently, some will conclude that the church holds the Bible in low esteem.

When visiting a Jewish synagogue service or attending the Divine Liturgy of the Greek Orthodox Church, one is always impressed with the reverence that surrounds the reading of the Word. It is all done with such a sense of caring and devotion; even a stranger can detect that

Stan Sadowski

something profound is happening. Although the Lutheran church is known as the church of the Bible and has a high doctrine of the Word, our worship practices do not always reflect such a boast. This is especially true when lectors read from the back of the church, or read from a flimsy lectionary insert or paperback book, or use a paraphrase of the Bible, or have the congregation read the lessons in unison. The church and the Word of God deserve better treatment.

Consider the following suggestions: After the congregation responds to the Prayer of the Day by saying the Amen, the reader of the First Lesson walks to the place of reading. The reader bows toward the altar, praying for God's help, and then makes sure that the Bible or lectionary is open to the right page. With a firm and clear voice, the lector announces the reading as the LBW rubrics suggest:

"The First Lesson is from the ______ chapter of ______." There is no need to embellish this brief, succinct, and adequate announcement. Nor is there a need to indicate the verses that are included in the reading; the people are expected to give full attention to the *hearing* of the Word and will not be "following along" as they would in a study class. And it is sufficient to let the Word speak for itself, making it unnecessary to tell the people what they are about to hear. It will be the sermon's task to provide the explanations and interpretations that need to be made.

Then the lector begins to read the Word of God with clarity, fully prepared to pronounce each word correctly and being sure that all will hear each word. While all eyes focus on the reader and all ears hungrily claim what is being read, the lector gives full attention to the printed words that are being read. Attempting to establish eye contact with the hearers during the reading is not only unnecessary, it also distracts attention from a full concentration on the reading.

When the assigned reading concludes, the lector may say "Here ends the reading" and then should prepare the book for the Second Lesson by turning to the proper page. Then, bowing toward the altar in gratitude for the privilege of proclaiming God's Word, the lector returns to his or her seat.

THE PSALM

The three assigned readings in the liturgy are interspersed with two biblical songs: the Psalm and the Verse. These biblical songs are part of the liturgy of the Word. As such, these songs support and reflect the three readings and help communicate that part of God's story which is being celebrated that day.

Psalms are hymns; by being sung, they achieve their intended use. Ten Psalm tones are provided for this purpose on page 291 of the *Lutheran Book of Worship*. Since it is often the assisting minister's assignment as cantor to lead the singing of the appointed Psalm, it is helpful to be aware of the several methods of using the Psalms. Varying the methods, perhaps according to the seasons of the church year, may help enhance the liturgy and prevent monotony. These methods include the following:

1. Direct recitation: The Psalm, or its appointed portion, is sung or read in unison. Prior to the Psalm, the antiphon melody is played by the organist, and then the cantor or choir sings the antiphon *a cappella*. The congregation then repeats the antiphon with organ accompaniment. After the Psalm is completed, the antiphon is repeated by all.
2. Antiphonal recitation: Groups of singers or readers alternate by whole verses. This may involve alternation between choir/cantor and congregation, between two sides of the congregation, between men and women, and so forth. The Psalm is preceded and followed by its antiphon, as detailed in #1. Antiphonal recitation is recommended when long Psalms are appointed.
3. Responsorial recitation: The verses of the Psalm are sung by the cantor or choir, with the congregation singing the antiphon as a refrain between groups of verses.
4. Responsive recitation: The Psalm is read in verse-by-verse alternation between an assisting minister and the congregation. The antiphon is sung as in #1.

As the last verse of the Psalm is being sung, the reader of the Second Lesson quietly and unobtrusively walks to the place of the reading.

THE SECOND LESSON

Pausing first to bow toward the altar, the lector determines that the book is open to the correct page for the reading. The Second Lesson is then announced and read and concluded by the lector, guided by the rubrics of the liturgy and by the counsel offered above in the section on the First Lesson.

The lector will need to know what has been planned for the next reading, the Holy Gospel. Is the book to be handed to the preacher of the day? Should the book be given to the bookbearer for a Gospel procession? Is the book to be carried by the lector to some other place of reading? Since the reading of the Holy Gospel is regarded as a major event in the celebration of the liturgy, all worship leaders will need to be aware of what is to happen during the singing of the Verse in preparation for that reading.

VERSE

Following the reading of the Second Lesson, all stand in anticipation of the reading of the Gospel. A biblical song called the Verse serves as a processional hymn for the one who goes to the place where the Gospel will be proclaimed. Usually, it is only the preacher of the day in that procession, and the Gospel probably will be read at the same place at which the sermon will be preached.

On some festival occasions, the book of the Gospels will be carried in solemn procession during the singing of the Verse to the place of reading. Such a procession may include the crucifer with cross, the torchbearers with lighted candles, the bookbearer with Bible or lectionary, and the reader. This procession may lead to the front of the center aisle or it may go into the midst of the assembly. At whatever place it occurs, all worshipers turn to face the reader, standing to honor Christ the Word coming into the midst of the congregation.

The Verse sung between the Second Lesson and the announcement of the Gospel should be the one appointed for the day. It is sung by the choir or by a single voice—an assisting minister (cantor) or someone in the choir. In order that more of the biblical message can be heard by the people, the appointed verses for each Sunday are preferred over the two general verses provided as congregational alternates.

Ralph R. Van Loon

S. Anita Stauffer

THE HOLY GOSPEL AND SERMON

Tradition and theology have ascribed to the reading of the Gospel a prominent position in the liturgy. These are the words which are related to the birth, ministry, death, and resurrection of Jesus Christ. Under no circumstances would such words be omitted from any celebration of the liturgy. The reading of the Holy Gospel is not governed by a permissive rubric; it is insisted upon. These words are so important to the church that the reading of the Holy Gospel is surrounded by liturgical practices not granted to the other readings. Those who have leadership roles during this part of the service need to be aware of the special character of these moments and strive to let that character have full expression.

When the Verse is concluded and the Gospel reader is in place, and all the people have turned to face the book, the announcement is made by the reader: "The Holy Gospel according to St. _______, the __ chapter." It's the announcement for which all have waited, and the congregation shouts its acclamation song: "Glory to you, O Lord."

And, as the reader fills the church with the words of the appointed Gospel, every ear and eye is at full and reverent attention. No head is bowed, buried in the bulletin. No mind permits diverting thoughts. No eye roves to see who is in attendance. No ear shuts out the sounds of the words. Only the head of the reader is turned downward, enabling the eyes to follow and deliver each and every word on that sacred page. Again, the reader makes no attempt to establish eye contact with the hearers; the reader's only assignment is to proclaim the words of the Gospel reading to the assembly—and when that assignment is completed, to lift head and eyes and voice, declaring firmly and gratefully that what all have heard is truly "The Gospel of the Lord." Because these words of Christ's good news always bring counsel and hope, the congregation shouts yet another acclamation song: "Praise to you, O Christ."

If there has been a Gospel procession into the nave, the crucifer leads the procession group back toward the sanctuary, and the preacher for the day continues the proclamation of God's Word through the sermon. It is the preacher's task to make clear the relevance and pertinence of the Word for the life and mission of the people. Except in very rare instances, such an assignment is filled only by one who has been called to the ministry of the Word through ordination. Assisting ministers should give full attention to the preacher during the sermon. This is a time to listen with full concentration.

The rubrics encourage a time of silence following the sermon. During this time, all present are seated with eyes closed and heads bowed. No sounds are heard: no "background music," no turning of pages, no walking about, no fidgeting in chancel or nave. It is the time to hear that unique sound which can only be heard in silence—the still, small voice of God. Such a voice will be difficult to hear if the time of silence is only a brief bit of ritualistic perfunctoriness. Through their own full and devout use of this time of reflection and meditation, worship leaders will help the congregation discover the value and benefit of liturgical silence. (A similar time of silence is provided during the Brief Order for Confession and Forgiveness and again just before the presiding minister gives the Benediction.) Liturgically, silence is always golden.

HYMN OF THE DAY

This hymn is quite unlike all others that may be included in the service. This is regarded as the major hymn of the service because it is one of the proclamatory parts of the liturgy. This hymn is always selected on the basis of its relationship to the appointed lessons and Gospel. The distinctive nature and role of this hymn is also apparent in the way the parish musicians introduce, accompany, and lead it. Since all will stand to sing this hymn, worship leaders will need to agree when the silence following the sermon is to conclude and when the congregation is to stand for the Hymn of the Day. In most situations, when the presiding minister stands, that is an adequate signal for the other worship leaders and the congregation to stand. (Similarly, when the presiding minister sits down, it is a signal for the assisting ministers and the congregation to be seated. It should not be necessary to resort to hand signals or verbal instructions for the congregation to know whether to stand or sit during any part of the liturgy.)

THE CREED

The rubrics do not require the use of a Creed at each celebration of the liturgy. In most cases, however, one of the Creeds will be included (the Apostles' Creed on "green Sundays," and the Nicene Creed on other Sundays), and the presiding minister will be expected to lead it. The assisting minister may hold the book for the presider during the Creed.

THE PRAYERS

The assisting minister leads the congregation's intercessions. Through the reading and preaching of the Word of God, the people sense the need to seek God's intervention in those distresses and challenges which confront the parish, the wider Church, and the world. While much of the liturgy is devoted to the offering of prayers, these particular petitions are characterized by their explicit intent to seek God's help and blessing upon all sorts and conditions of humankind. As such, these intercessions are as pointed and pertinent as the day's news. Specific mention should be made of persons, places, and predicaments in the world, the nation, the community, and the parish. Of special concern will be the Church in every place, its leaders and people, its life and mission.

These prayers are prepared by the presiding and assisting ministers. While each petition expresses the note of immediacy, each must be carefully worded. Such work begins early in the week, shaping each petition with the kind of flexibility that enables the addition or revision of specific references as may be necessary. If the news on Saturday evening discloses the fact that a disaster has occurred, the assisting minister needs to be ready to include such a reference in The Prayers. By the same token, be prepared to alter a petition for healing if the person died during the night. (See work sheet, page 43.)

The petitions should be brief and to the point, avoiding homiletical character. The prayers should be corporate in character and spirit. Each petition usually ends with "let us pray to the Lord" (to which the congregation responds, "Lord, have mercy") or "Lord, in your mercy" (with the congregation responding "hear our prayer"). Lengthy recitations by the assisting minister are thus avoided.

Before reading the petitions of The Prayers, the assisting minister should be sure about the pronunciation of names of the various persons and places that are to be mentioned. If necessary, write out the name phonetically. Family members dislike hearing the names of their loved ones incorrectly pronounced. It is traditional and preferable to use only first names in The Prayers, providing the full names in the bulletin or announcements.

The last petition of the assisting minister is a thanksgiving or commemoration of the faithful departed. Here it is appropriate to name persons who have recently died, as well as persons commemorated that day in the church year calendar (such as Michelangelo on April 6, St. Mary Magdalene on July 22, and Ambrose on December 7).

It is the presiding minister's task to conclude The Prayers. The LBW liturgy provides a text of commendation for this purpose.

S. Anita Stauffer

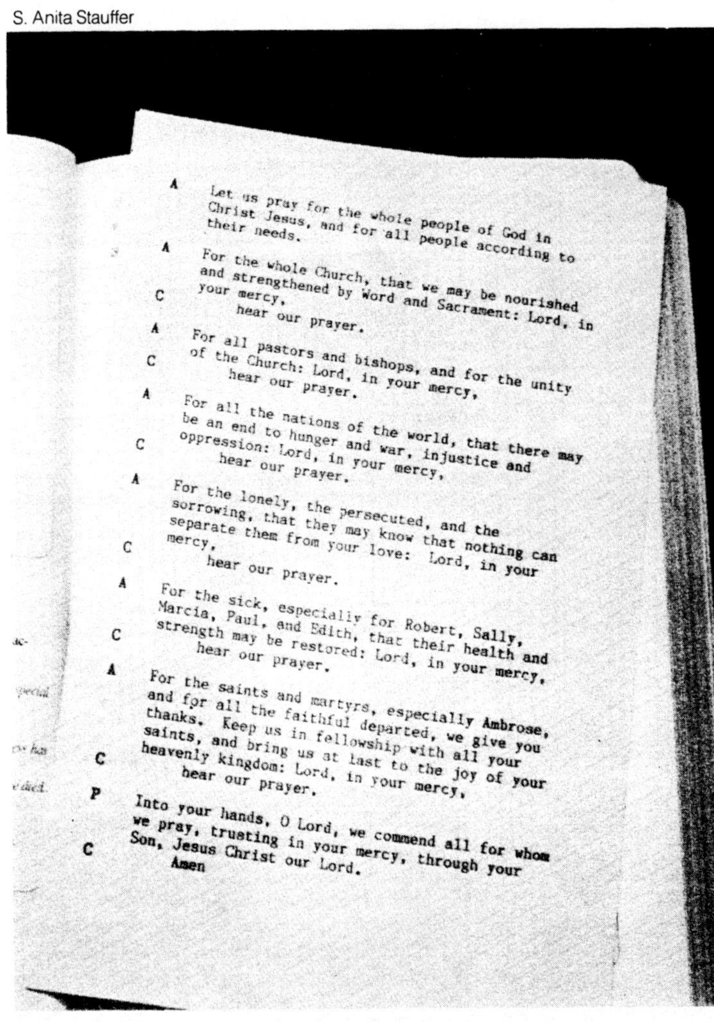

A Let us pray for the whole people of God in Christ Jesus, and for all people according to their needs.

A For the whole Church, that we may be nourished and strengthened by Word and Sacrament: Lord, in your mercy,
C hear our prayer.

A For all pastors and bishops, and for the unity of the Church: Lord, in your mercy,
C hear our prayer.

A For all the nations of the world, that there may be an end to hunger and war, injustice and oppression: Lord, in your mercy,
C hear our prayer.

A For the lonely, the persecuted, and the sorrowing, that they may know that nothing can separate them from your love: Lord, in your mercy,
C hear our prayer.

A For the sick, especially for Robert, Sally, Marcia, Paul, and Edith, that their health and strength may be restored: Lord, in your mercy,
C hear our prayer.

A For the saints and martyrs, especially Ambrose, and for all the faithful departed, we give you thanks. Keep us in fellowship with all your saints, and bring us at last to the joy of your heavenly kingdom: Lord, in your mercy,
C hear our prayer.

P Into your hands, O Lord, we commend all for whom we pray, trusting in your mercy, through your Son, Jesus Christ our Lord.
C Amen

THE PEACE

Following the example of our Lord after his resurrection, the presiding minister speaks the words of the Peace. These words transport the congregation into that part of the service which is the climax of the liturgy, the Holy Communion. The Peace constitutes a most solemn prayer that all present will be granted that divine gift which passes all understanding. These are words of baptismal unity, reconciliation, mutual acceptance, and common resolve to work together in mission—a response to the Gospel, in preparation for the holy Meal.

While the words of the Peace possess strength and significance in and of themselves, a ritual action is called for to reinforce the words and to make clear their meaning. For this reason, when the presiding minister has spoken the Peace, the sign of Peace is then exchanged with the assisting minister. This sign of Peace could be a simple handshake, a form of greeting that is quite common throughout much of the world. The Christians of the early church had their own form of exchanging the Peace—they called it the holy kiss (1 Corinthians 16:20). If a kiss seems not to be appropriate and if a handshake seems less than adequate for this solemn moment, perhaps an embrace could become the congregation's sign of Peace.

The presiding minister and assisting minister can do much to set the tone for this profound moment in the liturgy. With books put aside, these worship leaders should greet one another with solemn warmth and cordiality, speaking directly to each other the words of the Peace, embracing one another with the sign of Peace. This becomes a signal for all present to address one another with the words and sign of the Peace. The presiding and assisting ministers reach out to the other ministers and then to others present in the nave. It is not intended that the ministers will go up and down the aisles, reaching every row of seats in the nave. Instead, these ministers are encouraged to reach toward those who are somewhat nearby.

"Peace be with you" are the words that are spoken during the exchange of the Peace. Using other greetings and engaging in other kinds of conversation will obscure and trivialize the meaning of these moments in the liturgy. Other such greetings may be exchanged when the liturgy concludes.

Ralph R. Van Loon

PREPARING FOR THE EUCHARIST

Following the exchange of the Peace, the presiding minister is seated, the ushers prepare to receive the money offering, and the assisting minister goes to the altar to make it ready for the sacramental Meal.

All that has been said and done thus far in the liturgy has been a preparation for what now follows. Throughout the liturgy of the Word, the congregation has given attention to the will and promises of God. What we can count on from God and what God expects of us have been the gifts and concerns of that first part of the liturgy. But now the liturgy will assume quite a different character as it engages the congregation in that ritual Meal which our Lord instituted for life and salvation with him and all his saints.

Because the assisting minister has a significant leadership role in the celebration of that holy Supper, it is imperative that there be more than just a casual awareness of what this Meal is. While it is true that the common elements of bread and wine are used for this Meal, there is nothing common about their identity when given to the communicant. What is given during this part of the liturgy is the very, and true, and real Body and Blood of Christ. Assisting ministers will handle and serve such sacred species. These leaders will become instruments of the Holy Spirit as the lives of the faithful are mystically joined to the person and life of Christ. They become the administrators of God's saving and renewing grace, that divine gift which nourishes, encourages, and sustains the baptized people of God.

It is no wonder that the Church has always surrounded this part of the liturgy with great reverence and devotion. A mystery is being confronted here. The whole "Church on earth and the hosts of heaven" are assembled in this place of Holy Communion. A glimpse of the glory and majesty of God is granted in *this* place. And the Lord Christ, who promised to be with us always, gives an intensity to that promise through the assurances of "this is my Body, given for you." A mystery is unfolding here, and the assisting minister becomes one of the stewards of that mystery. Such an awareness will shape the attitude, deportment, and leadership style of all those who serve at the altar of the Blessed Sacrament.

THE OFFERING

While the money offerings of the people are being gathered, the assisting minister approaches the front of the altar, bows toward it, then stands at the altar to prepare it for the celebration of the Holy Communion.

The LBW encourages congregations to provide an altar that is freestanding, one that permits the presiding minister to stand behind the altar and to face the people during the Great Thanksgiving. Such an arrangement was typical for church buildings for the first several centuries of Christianity. Later in the Middle Ages, when the liturgy became a clergy specialty, the altar was placed against the wall. In 1526, Martin Luther urged churches to return to the earlier practice: ". . . the priest should always face the people as Christ doubtlessly did in the Last Supper."[1] This arrangement enables people to discover the meal character of the Eucharist and permits all present to have a greater intimacy with the actions which accompany the eucharistic liturgy.

Whatever its position, freestanding or against the chancel wall, the altar should be thirty-nine inches high; the other dimensions will be influenced by the architecture of the chancel and nave. Every altar is expected to have at least two coverings: one covering which has the same dimensions as the mensa (the top surface of the altar), is called a *cerecloth* and provides a kind of padding and protection for the fair linen. The *fair linen* covers the entire mensa and is long enough to hang over each end of the altar, perhaps twelve inches from the floor. It is customary for Lutherans to give further honor to the altar by the addition of a parament in the color of the season or festival of the church year. At least two candles also adorn the altar. Altar flowers are placed on the retable of east-wall altars; flowers are not usually placed on freestanding altars. Because they give the suggestion of empty sacrifices, empty vases and empty offering plates are never placed on an altar. The missal stand and altar book (*LBW Ministers Edition*) are placed on the altar just before a service and removed when the service concludes. Placing open Bibles on the mensa for decoration is not a part of Lutheran tradition and serves no purpose.

Because of a diversity of practices regarding methods of celebrating and distributing Holy Communion among our parishes, the following options are possible:

A. At the altar, the principal assisting minister opens the altar book to the Offertory Prayer. At the same time, another assisting minister (or acolyte) goes to the credence table (or shelf), picks up the folded corporal linen, and carries it to the altar where it is given to the assisting minister who will spread it on the mensa. The corporal, folded to make nine equal squares, is opened and unfolded on the mensa with the fold creases pointing downward. The corporal is placed at the center of the mensa, its hem aligned with the nearest edge of the mensa. This square linen is a kind of "place mat" on which the sacramental vessels and elements will be placed.

While the corporal is being spread, purificators are brought from the credence to be handed to the assisting minister. Next to be brought to the altar from the credence is the empty chalice covered with a pall. If more than one chalice will be needed, it is not brought to the altar until it is time to begin the distribution. At that time it will be filled with wine from the flagon or cruet at the altar.

1. Ulrich S. Leupold, ed. *Luther's Works*, 53, *Liturgy and Hymns* (Philadelphia: Fortress Press, 1965), 69.

B. At the altar, the assisting minister opens the altar book to the Offertory Prayer, then walks to the credence table (or shelf) to pick up the vested chalice. At the altar, the vested chalice is placed on the right side of the mensa. The corporal is removed from the burse; the burse is set aside while the corporal is unfolded on its place on the mensa, with all creases pointing downward. After the corporal is in place, the chalice is set on it. The chalice veil is lifted carefully from the chalice, folded, and set near the burse. The chalice pall is set to one side; the paten with host is lifted from the chalice and placed on the mensa near the edge of the altar; the purificator on the chalice is removed and placed on the right edge of the corporal; and finally the chalice pall is replaced on the empty chalice. Additional purificators may then be brought to the altar from the credence by the acolyte.

S. Anita Stauffer

C. If individual Communion glasses will be used, they should not be prefilled with wine. Instead, a chalice with a pouring lip should be provided, and communicants each receive an empty Communion glass from a tray as they approach the Communion rail. Because Lutherans have a high concept of the Sacrament, it is not seemly to use disposable Communion glasses.

THE OFFERTORY

In each of the options described above, it has been assumed that the Offertory procession includes bread and wine as well as money gifts. Such a procession implies that a small table, holding the flagon or cruets of wine and the paten or pyx or ciborium of Communion bread, had been placed near the nave entrance. When the money offering has been gathered, the Offertory procession forms at the back of the center aisle. As the Offertory begins, the congregation stands and the ushers bear the money gifts toward the altar. Behind the ushers, walking single file, is a member of the congregation carrying the bread for Communion and another member carrying the wine.

In the chancel, the ushers deliver the offering plates to an acolyte, who hands them across the altar to the assisting minister or who slightly lifts the plates in a gesture of presentation and then places them on the credence. The ushers then step to either side of the aisle to permit the one bearing bread to hand the paten or ciborium or pyx across the altar to the assisting minister, who places it on the corporal between the chalice and the nearest edge of the altar. Then the wine is similarly presented to the assisting minister, who places the flagon or cruet at the upper right hand corner of the corporal. The ushers and Offertory presenters then return to their places.

A whole loaf of bread is preferable to wafers (hosts), both because it makes clearer the meal character of the Eucharist and because the whole loaf is a sign of unity: "Because there is one bread, we who are many are one body, for we all partake of the one bread" (1 Corinthians 10:17). The wine should be a dinner wine (not sweet) made from grapes. It may be red or white, although red stains are more difficult to remove from the linens.

THE OFFERTORY PRAYER

The rubrics direct that the assisting minister lead the congregation in one of the Offertory Prayers provided in the liturgy. It is appropriate for the assisting minister to have hands raised in the orans posture of prayer during

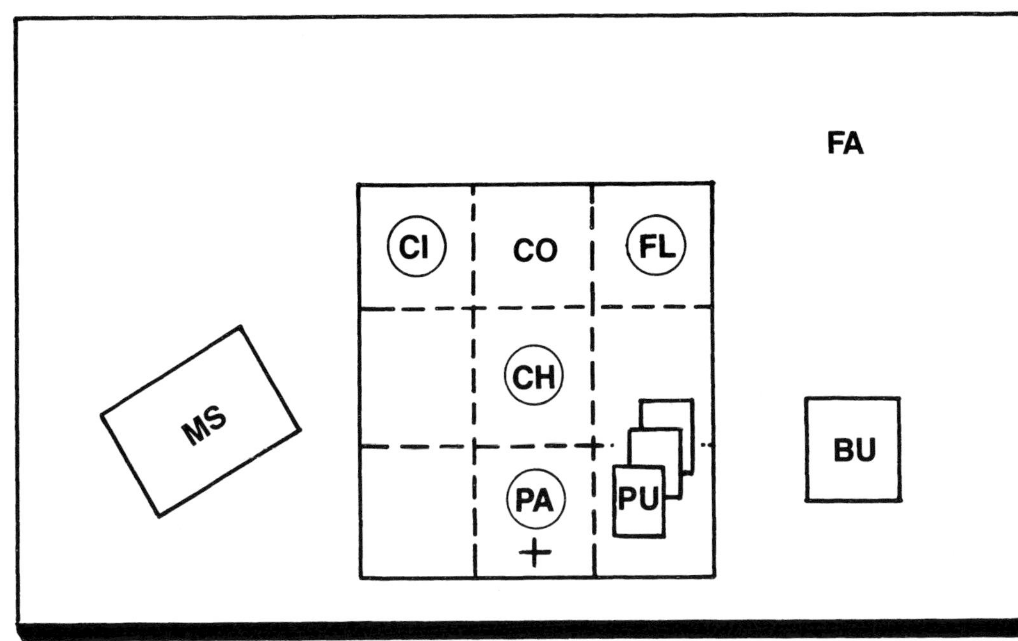

BU Burse
CH Chalice
CI Ciborium or Host Box
CO Corporal
FA Fair Linen
FL Flagon or Cruet
MS Missal Stand
PA Paten
PU Purificators

(If a whole loaf of bread is used, the ciborium or host box is omitted.)

this part of the liturgy. At the conclusion of the Offertory Prayer, the assisting minister pours wine into the chalice, holding a purificator near the spout of the flagon or cruet to prevent the wine from being spilled on the corporal or fair linen.

PREFACE AND EUCHARISTIC PRAYER

After the assisting minister has poured wine from the flagon into the chalice and has stepped aside, the presiding minister approaches the altar. The presiding minister's liturgical identity as a sign of Christ is never more evident than during the Great Thanksgiving: For this part of the service, the assisting minister stands to one side of the presiding minister, at a position near the altar book. At such a position, the assisting minister can oversee the book, turning pages as necessary, and assisting the presider as requested. The assisting minister joins the congregation in the responses during the Preface Dialog and Eucharistic Prayer, and in singing the *Sanctus*. It is customary to bow profoundly during the *Sanctus* (through the first "Hosanna in the highest"), as we recall with awe Isaiah's vision of God's majesty, and to make the sign of the cross during the words "Blessed is he who comes in the name of the Lord."

THE FRACTION

Following the praying of the Lord's Prayer, the presiding minister breaks the bread in anticipation of the distribution.

THE COMMUNION

The presiding minister, making clear a love for and a dependence upon this Means of Grace, is the first to receive the Holy Communion. The assisting ministers then present themselves to the presiding minister to

S. Anita Stauffer

receive their own communions while the congregation sings the *Agnus Dei* or some other appropriate hymn. It is customary, when about to receive the Body of Christ, to trace upon oneself the sign of the cross and to extend the palm of the right hand to the minister with the left hand directly under the right as support. This positioning of hands helps form a "throne" on which the holy Bread is placed. Both hands are then brought to the mouth, and the bread is consumed. After receiving the bread, the communicant may bow the head and say softly, "Amen" and "the Lord's Body and my body."

When the chalice is offered, the communicant should grasp the base of the chalice to assist the minister in lifting the cup to the lips. After receiving the wine, communicants may trace upon themselves the sign of the cross and say softly, "Amen" and "the Lord's Blood and my life." As the assisting minister and the other ministers exercise these customs with reverence and sincerity, others in the congregation can capture a keener awareness that the moments of Communion are supremely profound.

If additional chalices are needed for the Communion, they are now brought from the credence to the altar and are filled with the wine in the flagon. Then the presiding minister hands the sacramental vessels to those who will serve as eucharistic ministers. It is the presider's assignment to distribute the Body of Christ to communicants; the assisting minister offers the Blood of Christ to the communicants.

A purificator is always used with a chalice. After each communicant receives the Sacrament, the rim is wiped and the chalice is turned. A purificator is also used with a pouring lip chalice; then the purificator is held directly below the pouring spout to prevent dripping or spillage.

Most chalices are made with a node in the stem. This enables the Communion minister to lock the index and middle fingers about the chalice stem for ease in ministration and to maintain necessary stability and leverage during ministration.

Adequate distance between the ministers of the bread and the cup needs to be maintained. Normally, if three communicants separate these two ministers, an appearance of being rushed is avoided.

The church expects the Communion ministers to deal personally and reverently with each individual communicant. For this reason, the rubrics direct that as the bread and cup are given, these words are said to each person receiving Communion:

> "The body of Christ, given for you."
>
> "The blood of Christ, shed for you."

This formula should not be altered. Eye contact should be established with the communicant as these words are spoken. These words make it clear that a wondrous gift is being given to each individual member of the royal priesthood of believers.

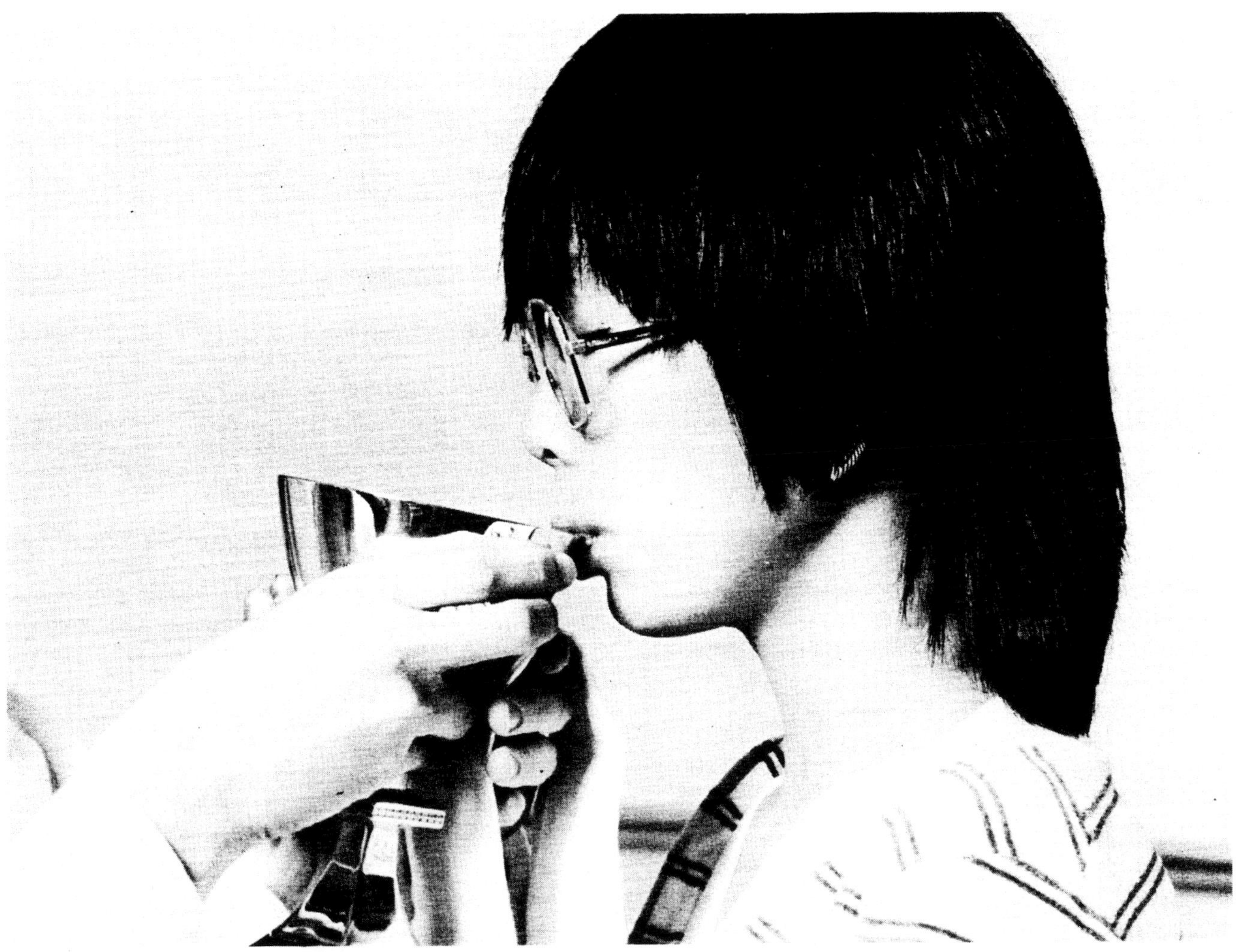

Stan Sadowski

POST-COMMUNION

When all have received, the ministers return to the altar. The presiding minister speaks the Post-Communion Blessing. Then, while the congregation sings a canticle or hymn of thanksgiving, the presiding minister steps aside and the assisting minister clears the Table. Among the options for this procedure are these:

A. The bread that remains is returned to its vessel and handed to another assisting minister, perhaps an acolyte, who places it on the credence table. Each chalice is similarly placed on the credence and covered with a pall or purificator. The flagon is removed to the credence; then the purificators are removed. The assisting minister carefully refolds the corporal while it is on the mensa and then hands it to the other assisting minister or acolyte who places it on the credence.

B. The bread that remains is returned to the ciborium by the presiding minister, who places it in the aumbry or hands it to the assisting minister for placement on the credence. The presiding minister may consume the wine remaining in the chalice, cleanse it, and then step aside to allow the assisting minister to complete the clearing of the Table. First to be removed are the flagon and all extra purificators. Then the assisting minister places purificator, paten, and pall on the chalice and covers it with the chalice veil. The covered chalice is then placed to the right of the corporal. The corporal, carefully folded, is placed in the burse. The burse is placed on the chalice and carried to the credence.

C. If individual Communion glasses have been used during the distribution, communicants may place their used glasses in trays that have been set on small tables located near the entrance to the chancel.

After the altar has been cleared of all sacramental linens and vessels, the assisting minister turns to the proper page in the altar book and, when the canticle or hymn is concluded, stands to the side of the presiding minister and says to the congregation, "Let us pray." Then, with hands lifted, the assisting minister offers one of the three Post-Communion Prayers. The rubrics also permit the use of the second Prayer of the Day for Maundy Thursday as a Post-Communion Prayer.

SILENCE

Silence follows the Post-Communion Prayer, giving all present an opportunity to ponder the implications of the Holy Communion. In this place, heaven and earth have intersected. In this place, and about this altar, this congregation has joined the apostles and martyrs and all the saints to offer solemn adoration to the Most High, the God and Father of us all. In this place, a glimpse of God's glory has been perceived, forgiveness has been received, and the people have feasted at the Banquet of life and salvation. These are the thoughts that engage and refresh the assembly during the silence as all await the Benediction.

BENEDICTION AND DISMISSAL

The presiding minister, standing before the assembly in the stead of Christ, gives to all the blessing of Almighty God. All have turned toward the presider for the blessing. Every head has been bowed. Every hand and foot has been stilled, and every heart has been opened to receive this further outpouring of divine love and mercy. Then, as a glad indicator that such a rich blessing is accepted and treasured, all may trace the sign of the cross upon themselves as the presiding minister traces the cross over the entire assembly.

The liturgy now comes quickly to an end. It is not unlike the experience on the mount of the Ascension, when the disciples who witnessed that miracle did not want to leave that holy place. Angels appeared at that moment, diverting the disciples' attention from the sublimity of that divine encounter to the tasks awaiting them elsewhere (Acts 1:11). In the celebration of the liturgy, it is the assisting minister's role to remind the assembly that it is time to stop "looking into heaven" and to get on with our priesthood in the world. The assisting minister dismisses the congregation to "Go in peace. Serve the Lord." Such instruction is spoken with cordial firmness. All have heard it, and all sense the urgency of the assignment given. A kind of restlessness sweeps over the assembly, springing from an awareness that the world desperately needs our discipleship. The people get the last word; they respond to the assisting minister's instruction by shouting the Church's favorite words, "Thanks be to God."

The liturgy has told the people to "go," and now nothing should delay their going—not a hymn, not a sung benediction by the choir, not a candle-extinguishing ceremony, not softly played chimes, not announcements, not even silence. Instead, following the shout of "Thanks be to God," the procession of ministers should quickly form, leading the congregation from nave to narthex and to the waiting world.

Customarily, the presiding and assisting ministers greet the congregation in the narthex following the liturgy. Ordained ministers wearing stoles remove them before these greetings begin; the presiding minister also removes the chasuble. One of the acolytes could be recruited to carry these vestments to the sacristy.

AFTER THE SERVICE

After greeting the congregation, it is appropriate to gather in the sacristy (before removing the other vestments) for a brief prayer of thanksgiving, giving praise to God for the opportunity to serve as stewards of his holy mysteries, praying that the good seed of the Gospel will take root in the lives of all those who worship. A prayer such as the following may be used:

> Almighty God, you provide the true bread from heaven, your Son, Jesus Christ our Lord. Grant that we who have received the Sacrament of his body and blood may abide in him and he in us, that we may be filled with the power of his endless life, now and forever. Amen (LBW, page 48)

> Almighty God, grant that the words we have heard this day with our ears may be grafted onto our hearts through your grace, that they may produce in us the fruit of a good life, to the praise and honor of your name, through Jesus Christ, your Son our Lord. Amen (LBW, page 48)

> Almighty God, grant that we, who have been redeemed from the old life of sin by our baptism into the death and resurrection of your Son Jesus Christ, may be renewed in your Holy Spirit to live in righteousness and true holiness; through Jesus Christ our Lord. Amen (LBW, page 47)

Much yet remains to be done before all ministers and acolytes leave. If bread from a whole loaf remains and if wine remains in the chalice, these sacramental elements should be consumed by the ministers. If an inordinate quantity of wine remains in the chalice, it may be poured upon the ground or into the piscina. If it is parish custom, wine from the flagon and bread may be prepared for distribution to the sick and homebound. Otherwise, wine in the flagon is kept separate from wine which has not been consecrated.

In addition, the altar book and missal stand should be removed from the altar, the candles extinguished, bulletins discarded, attendance recorded, service books replaced, Communion vessels cleansed and stored, vestments returned to their places, the money offering counted and banked, the altar flowers delivered to the sick and shut-ins, soiled linens set aside for laundering, and the lights turned off. In most parishes, several people share these tasks, making it unnecessary for the assisting minister to do them all. However, common courtesy suggests that the assisting minister and acolytes seek ways to be helpful before leaving.

STUDY AND TRAINING

It is not enough just to read this handbook to become an effective assisting minister; much more is required. Study and training and practice are all necessary ingredients as one prepares to serve as a liturgical leader. None of these ingredients should be slighted; none should be omitted.

It is recommended that parishes provide study sessions for those who will serve as assisting ministers. Rather than designing a series of formal lectures, the pastor may find it more productive and helpful to arrange times of conversation and demonstration with those who will be designated as lay liturgical leaders. The following outline may be considered.

Session I: A Bit of Worship History

- A. Old Testament examples
  - 1. Tabernacle
  - 2. Temple
  - 3. Synagogue
- B. Christian liturgy in formation
  - 1. The Upper Room: four actions
    - a. Took
    - b. Blessed
    - c. Broke
    - d. Gave
  - 2. Emmaus
    - a. Christ opened to them the Scriptures
    - b. Their eyes were opened at the breaking of the bread
  - 3. Liturgy of the Word (from the synagogue)
  - 4. Liturgy of the Meal (from the Upper Room)
- C. Common expectations
  - 1. Gathering with other believers
  - 2. Remembering the mighty acts of God
  - 3. Receiving guidance, nourishment, blessing
  - 4. Offering the sacrifices of praise and thanksgiving

Session II: Worship Through the Centuries

- A. Cultic life of the early church
  - 1. Word and Sacrament
  - 2. An emerging church year calendar
  - 3. Processions, lights, sign of the cross, and so forth
  - 4. From house church to church buildings
- B. Medieval dilemmas
  - 1. Clergy/laity separation
  - 2. Infrequent reception of Holy Communion
  - 3. Liturgy as a clergy specialty
  - 4. Worship becomes a meritorious work
  - 5. Use of a "foreign" language for worship
- C. Lutheranism
  - 1. Reform, not revolution (see *The Augsburg Confession,* Article XXIV)
  - 2. Stress on participation: music, language, Communion
- D. Minimalism
  - 1. Lutheran liturgical and sacramental life challenged by 18th- and 19th-century movements
    - a. Pietism
    - b. Rationalism
    - c. Revivalism
  - 2. Much of Lutheranism in North America without traditional forms and practices
    - a. Little or no liturgy
    - b. Lutheran chorales often replaced by revival songs
    - c. Holy Communion celebrated once or twice a year
- E. Since middle of 19th century
  - 1. Confessional renewal prompts a liturgical renewal
  - 2. 1888—North American Lutherans reclaim the basic Western Mass for their use
  - 3. *Service Book and Hymnal* and *Lutheran Book of Worship* represent significant developments in liturgical and sacramental maturation

Session III: Our Liturgical Heritage

- A. Linkages with early Christianity and early Lutheranism
- B. The church year calendar and lectionary
  - 1. Telling and celebrating the church's story
  - 2. The cycle of seasons, saints' days, and holy days
  - 3. Colors, practices, themes for the church year
- C. The church's liturgy
  - 1. Brief Order for Confession and Forgiveness
  - 2. Liturgy of the Word
  - 3. Liturgy of the Sacramental Meal
- D. Current emphases
  - 1. The corporate nature of worship
  - 2. Shared leadership
  - 3. Weekly Communion
  - 4. Increased use of ritual actions in the celebration and proclamation of the Gospel
- E. Spiritual life of assisting ministers
  - 1. Prayer and Bible study
  - 2. Regular corporate worship

Session IV: The Setting: Where Liturgy Happens

- A. The rooms
  - 1. Narthex
  - 2. Nave
  - 3. Chancel
  - 4. Sanctuary
  - 5. Sacristy
- B. The furnishings
  - 1. Altar
  - 2. Pulpit
  - 3. Font
  - 4. Credence
  - 5. Communion rail
  - 6. Sedilia
  - 7. Seating
  - 8. Organ console
  - 9. Prie-dieu
- C. The appointments
  - 1. Cross, crucifix, processional cross

2. Candles, processional torches, baptismal candle, paschal candle
3. Alms basin
4. Missal stand
5. Vases
6. Thurible

Session V: Linens, Vessels, Vesture

A. Linens
1. Cerecloth
2. Fair linen
3. Paraments
4. Baptismal towel
5. Corporal
6. Burse
7. Chalice veil
8. Chalice pall
9. Purificator
10. Funeral pall

B. Vessels
1. Chalice
2. Ciborium
3. Host box
4. Lavabo
5. Cruets/Flagon
6. Paten
7. Ewer
8. Oil stock
9. Spoon

C. Vestments
1. Cassock
2. Alb
3. Amice
4. Cincture
5. Stole
6. Chasuble
7. Surplice
8. Cotta
9. Cope
10. Baptismal garment

Session VI: Other Services and Their Rubrics

A. Holy Baptism
B. Affirmation of Baptism
C. Marriage
D. Burial of the Dead
E. The Prayer Offices
1. Morning Prayer
2. Evening Prayer
3. Prayer at the Close of the Day
4. The Litany
5. Responsive Prayer 1 and 2
F. Service of the Word
G. *Occasional Services* book

The next set of sessions is designed to provide the lay leader with information and instruction regarding liturgical leadership style. While the topics may seem quite basic and routine, it needs to be recognized that the one being instructed may possess a self-consciousness that transforms the simplest action into a challenge. Then, too, it should not be assumed that ritual actions are easily learned and executed. The aim of this set of training sessions is to enable the assisting minister to develop a style of liturgical leadership that is exercised with ease, with naturalness, and without self-consciousness.

Session VII: Learning to Walk

A. In the sanctuary
1. From sedilia to lectern and return
2. From sedilia to altar and credence
3. From altar to altar rail

B. In procession
1. From narthex to nave to sanctuary
2. For a Gospel procession

C. With vestments, with book, with chalice, with folded hands
D. Negotiating steps
E. The art of sitting and standing

Session VIII: Ritual Actions

A. Folded hands
B. Orans
C. Kneeling
D. Bowing
E. Sign of the cross
F. The Peace

Session IX: What Is Done: When and Where and How

A. Brief Order for Confession and Forgiveness
B. Procession
C. Entrance Rite
D. The readings, The Prayers, Peace
E. Setting the Table
F. The Communion
G. Clearing the Table
H. Post-Communion

Session X: Chanting

A. Kyrie
B. Hymn of Praise
C. Psalmody

RESOURCES

For the study sessions, it may be helpful to refer to the following resources. (See full citations in the bibliography.)

Session I:
Lutherans at Worship, pp. 41–44
With This Bread and Cup, pp. 4–7
The Lutheran Liturgy, pp. 1–50

Session II:
The Lutheran Liturgy, pp. 51–227

Session III:
Lutherans at Worship, pp. 29–59
With This Bread and Cup
Parish Worship Handbook, pp. 7–10
Manual on the Liturgy, pp. 1–77
Session IV:
Lutherans at Worship, pp. 25–29
Space for Worship
Altar Guild Handbook
Manual on the Liturgy, pp. 148–166
Session V:
Altar Guild Handbook
Manual on the Liturgy
Session VI:
Lutherans at Worship, pp. 60–83
Manual on the Liturgy, pp. 167–198, 263–301, 339–366
By Water and the Spirit
In Love and Faithfulness
Sessions VII–X:
Manual on the Liturgy
With This Bread and Cup
Parish Worship Handbook

The need to practice again and again needs to be stressed again and again! In most instances, after training, these practice sessions can be times for individual work, when the assisting minister is alone in the church and walks through each part of the liturgy, reading and chanting aloud all the assigned parts, retracing each step, acting out each ritual action. This kind of disciplined practice reflects a determination to be an effective liturgical leader. It also permits the assisting minister to build self-confidence and to grant the liturgy the kind of care that it deserves. It is helpful for the pastor to be present occasionally during practice, so that incorrect habits are not developed.

Study, training, practice—each parish should be prepared to provide each of these educational elements to each person who is asked to serve as a liturgical leader. To provide less is to produce less.

Coupled with the parish's program to instruct assisting ministers is the expectation that the liturgical leaders will be seeking the preparation, strength, and refreshment that comes from daily prayer and meditation and from worship through Word and Sacrament each week.

It is recommended that the church's liturgical calendar and lectionary form the basis of the assisting minister's devotional life. The *Lutheran Book of Worship* offers many resources for such devotions: the appointed prayers, psalms, and readings; prayer offices; special prayers; and hymns. Such practices help form a liturgical consciousness, they immerse the assisting minister in the church's cycle of prayer, and they heighten one's love for the worship of God.

It is the church's expectation that each assisting minister will be adequately instructed before any liturgical leadership role is exercised in the parish. It is the further expectation of the church that those assisting ministers who will also assist in the distribution of Holy Communion will be approved by the church council and be duly installed by the pastor during the parish liturgy. The order for the installation of assisting ministers is contained in the rite of "Recognition of Ministries in the Congregation," in *Occasional Services*, pages 143–145.

May each one who is granted the high privilege of serving at the altar during the celebration of the church's liturgy of praise and adoration sense and make manifest that here we are about holy and consequential tasks. To God be the glory.

LECTIONARY PRONUNCIATION GUIDE

Abana	AH-bah-nah
Abba	AH-bah
Abednego	ah-BED-nee-go
Abel-meholah	AY-bel-mi-HO-lah
Abiathar	uh-BY-uh-thar
Abihu	uh-BY-hew
Abilene	ah-bih-LEE-nee
Achaia	ah-KAY-yah
Agabus	AH-gah-bus
Ahaz	AY-haz
Ai	AY-eye
Akeldama	uh-KEL-deh-muh
Alpha	AL-fah
Alphaeus	al-FEE-us
Amalek	AM-ah-lek
Amalekites	ah-MAL-eh-kites
Amaziah	am-uh-ZY-uh
Ammonites	AM-uh-nites
Amorites	AM-oh-rites
Amos	AY-mus
Amoz	AY-muz
Amphipolis	am-FIPP-oh-lis
Ananias	an-ah-NY-us
Annas	ANN-as
Antioch	ANN-tee-ok
Apollos	ah-PAWL-lus
Appolonia	ap-puh-LOW-nee-ah
Apphia	AFF-ih-ah
Aram	AIR-am
Aramean	air-ah-MAY-an
Archippus	ar-KIPP-us
Arimathea	air-ih-math-EE-ah
Asherah	ah-SHE-rah
Asherim	ASH-uh-reem
Assyria	ah-SEER-ee-ah
Azariah	az-ah-RY-ah
Azotus	ah-ZOH-tus

Baal	BAY-uhl
Baal-zephon	BAY-uhl-ZEE-fon
Babylonia	bab-ih-LOW-nee-ah
Balaam	BAY-lam
Balak	BAY-lak
Barabbas	bah-RAH-bus
Barachiah	bar-ah-KY-ah
Barnabas	BAR-nah-bus
Barsabbas	bar-SAH-bus
Bartimaeus	bar-tih-MAY-us
Bashan	BAY-shan
Bdellium	DELL-ih-um
Beelzebub	bee-ELL-ze-bub
Beersheba	beer-SHEE-bah
Beor	BEE-or
Berakiah	bear-ah-KY-ah
Berea	beh-REE-ah
Bethel	BETH-el
Beth-peor	beth-PEE-ohr
Bethphage	BETH-fah-jee
Bethsaida	beth-SAY-ih-dah
Bithynia	bih-THIN-ee-ah

Caesarea	sehs-ah-REE-ah
Caiaphas	KAY-ah-fas
Calneh	KAL-neh
Canaan	KAY-nan
Candace	KAN-duh-see
Capernaum	kuh-PER-nee-um
Cappadocia	kah-puh-DOH-shee-uh
Cephas	SEE-fas
Chaldeans	kal-DEE-anz
Chilion	KILL-ee-on
Chloe	KLOH-ee
Cilicia	sih-LISH-ih-ah
Claudius	KLAW-dih-us
Cleopas	KLEE-oh-pas
Clopas	KLOH-pas
Colossae	koh-LAH-sih
Crescens	KRES-enz
Cretans	KREE-tuns
Cyrene	sy-REE-nee
Cyrenians	sy-REE-nee-ans

Dalmatia	dal-MAY-shih-ah
Decapolis	deh-KAPP-uh-lis
Demas	DEE-mas
Denarii	deh-NAIR-ee-ee
Didymus	DIH-dih-mus
Dura	DYOO-rah

Edom	EE-dum
Elam	EE-lam
Elamites	EE-lam-ights
Eldad	ELL-dad
Eli	EE-lie
Eliezer	ell-ih-EE-zer
Elimelech	eh-LIMM-eh-lek
Elkanah	el-KAY-nah
Eloi, Eloi, lama sabachthani	AY-loy, AY-loy, LAH-mah sah-bahk-THAH-nee
El Shaddai	ell SHAD-eye
Emmaus	eh-MAY-us
Epaphras	EH-pah-fras
Ephah	EE-fah
Ephesus	EFF-eh-sus
Ephphatha	EFF-ah-thah
Ephraim	EE-fray-im
Ephrathah	EF-rah-thah
Ephrathites	EF-rah-thights
Etham	EE-tham
Euphrates	yoo-FRAY-teez

Gabbatha	GAH-bah-thah
Galatia	gah-LAY-shah
Gaza	GAH-zah
Gennesaret	geh-NESS-eh-ret
Gihon	GUY-hon
Gilead	GILL-ee-add
Gilgal	GILL-gal
Golgotha	GOLL-goh-thah
Gomorrah	goh-MOR-ah

Habakkuk	hah-BAK-uk
Hades	HAY-deez
Hagar	HAY-gar
Hamath	HAY-math
Hananiah	han-ah-NY-ah
Haran	HAY-ran
Hazael	HAH-zah-ell
Hermes	HUR-meez
Horeb	HOR-eb
Hyssop	HIH-sup
Iconium	eye-KOH-nee-um
Iscariot	iss-KAIR-ee-ot
Ituraea	it-yur-EE-ah
Jabbok	JAB-ok
Jairus	JAI-rus
Japheth	JAY-feth
Jearim	JEE-eh-rim
Jehoiada	jeh-HOY-ah-dah
Jehoiakim	jeh-HOY-ah-kim
Jehu	JEE-hyoo
Jeroboam	jair-uh-BOH-am
Joash	JOH-ash
Joses	JOH-seez
Josiah	joh-SY-ah
Judah	JOO-dah
Judea	joo-DEE-ah
Justus	JUS-tus
Kadesh	KAY-desh
Kidron	KID-run
Laodicea	lay-oh-dih-SEE-ah
Levi	LEE-vy
Lucius	LOO-shus
Lycaonian	lik-ah-OH-nee-an
Lysanias	ly-SAY-nih-as
Lystra	LISS-trah
Macedonia	mass-eh-DOH-nee-ah
Magdala	MAG-dah-lah
Mahlon	MAH-luhn
Malchus	MAL-kus
Mamre	MAHM-ree
Manaen	MAN-ah-en
Manasseh	mah-NASS-eh
Massah	MASS-ah
Matthias	mah-THIGH-us
Medad	MEE-dad
Medes	MEEDZ
Media	MEE-dee-ah
Melchizedek	mel-KIZZ-eh-dek
Meribah	MAIR-ih-bah
Merran	MAIR-un
Meshach	MEE-shak
Mesopotamia	mess-oh-poh-TAY-mee-ah
Midian	MIH-dih-an
Migdol	MIG-doll
Mizar	MY-zar
Moab	MOH-ab
Moabite	MOH-ah-bite
Moreh	MOH-reh
Moriah	moh-RY-ah
Mysia	MISS-ee-ah
Naaman	NAY-ah-man
Nadab	NAY-dab
Naphtali	NAFF-tah-lie
Nebo	NEE-boh
Nebuchadnezzer	neh-buh-kuhd-NEH-zer
Negev	NEG-ev
Nicanor	ny-KAY-nor
Nicodemus	nik-oh-DEE-mus
Niger	NY-jer
Nimshi	NIM-shy
Nineveh	NIHN-eh-veh
Omega	oh-MAY-gah
Onesimus	oh-NES-ih-mus
Ophir	OH-fur
Orpah	OR-pah
Pamphylia	pam-FILL-ee-ah
Paphos	PAY-foss
Papyrus	pah-PY-rus
Parmenas	PAHR-mee-nas
Parthia	PARTH-ee-ah
Parthians	PARTH-ee-uns
Patmos	PATT-mos
Peniel	PEN-ih-el
Perga	PURR-gah
Pergamum	PURR-gah-mum
Phanuel	FAN-yoo-el
Pharaoh	FAIR-oh
Pharpar	FAR-per
Philemon	fie-LEE-mon
Philippi	FILL-ih-py
Philistia	fih-LISS-tee-ah
Philistines	fih-LISS-tinz
Phoenicia	feh-NISH-ih-ah
Phrygia	FRIH-jee-uh
Pi-hahiroth	py-ha-HY-roth
Pisgah	PIZZ-gah
Pishon	PY-shon
Pisidia	pih-SID-ee-ah
Pontus	PON-tus
Praetorium	pray-TOE-ree-um
Prochorus	PRAHK-oh-rus
Quirinius	kwih-RIN-ih-us
Rabboni	rah-BOH-ny
Rahab	RAY-hab
Ramah	RAY-mah
Rephidim	REF-ih-dim
Saba	SAY-bah
Sabaoth	SAB-ay-oth
Sadducees	SAD-yoo-seez
Salome	sah-LOH-mee

Sanhedrin	san-HEE-drin
Sardis	SAR-dis
Sepulchre	SEH-pull-kur
Shadrach	SHAD-rak
Shaphat	SHAY-fat
Shechem	SHEH-kum
Sheol	SHEE-ohl
Shiloh	SHY-loh
Shinar	SHY-nar
Shittim	SHIH-tim
Sidon	SY-duhn
Siloam	sih-LOH-am
Silvanus	sill-VAY-nus
Simeon	SIM-ee-un
Sinews	SIN-yooz
Smyrna	SMUR-nah
Sodom	SOD-um
Sosthenes	SAHS-theh-neez
Stephanas	STEFF-ah-nas
Succoth	SUKK-oth
Sycamine	SIK-eh-min
Sychar	SIH-ker
Syrophoenician	sy-roh-feh-NISH-an
Tabor	TAY-bor
Talitha cumi	TAL-ih-thah KOO-mee
Tarshish	TAR-shish
Teman	TEE-man
Terebinth	TAIR-eh-binth
Tetrarch	TEH-trark
Theophilus	thee-AH-fih-lus
Thessalonica	thess-ah-loh-NY-kah
Thyatira	thigh-ah-TY-rah
Tiberias	ty-BIHR-ee-us
Tigris	TY-griss
Timaeus	tih-MEE-us
Timon	TY-mon
Titus	TY-tus
Trachonitis	trak-oh-NY-tis
Trigon	TRY-gon
Troas	TROH-ahs
Tubal	TYOO-bal
Tyre	TIRE
Uriah	yoo-RY-ah
Uzziah	uh-ZY-ah
Yahweh	YAH-way
Zalmon	ZAL-mon
Zarephath	ZAIR-eh-fath
Zebedee	ZEB-eh-dee
Zebulun	ZEB-yuh-lun
Zechariah	zek-ah-RY-ah
Zerubbabel	zeh-RUB-ah-bel
Zoan	ZOH-an
Zoar	ZOH-ar

WORK SHEET FOR THE PRAYERS

THE PRAYERS

For ____

(Service and date)

Write petitions appropriate for the whole Church, the nations, those in need, local community and parish needs, and thanksgiving for the faithful departed. Balance a universal scope of Christian concern with specific congregational concerns. Avoid homiletical tendencies, keeping the prayers corporate in style and spirit.

A Let us pray for the whole people of God in Christ Jesus, and for all people according to their needs.

(1)

After each portion of the prayers:

A Lord, in your mercy,	*or*	**A** Let us pray to the Lord.
C Hear our prayer.		**C** Lord, have mercy.

(2)

(3)

(4)

(5)

P Into your hands, O Lord, we commend all for whom we pray, trusting in your mercy; through your Son, Jesus Christ our Lord.

C Amen

READING TECHNIQUES

There are at least three things to be concerned about in the actual practice of public reading: production, pace and emphasis.

There are several basic rules to tone production and projection. They all begin with the fact that a vocal tone is produced by a column of air coming from the lungs and causing the voice box to vibrate. If that column of air is weak or irregular, the sound cannot be strong. For the column of air to be strong and regular, it must be supported. This support comes from the diaphragm, that band of muscles below the lungs that provide the muscular undergirding for the lungs. For the diaphragm to do any good at all, one must be standing erect, so that the muscles can "pull in the stomach." Erect posture and diaphragm support are the first essentials to proper tone production.

The second essential is adequate quantities of air. This requires deep breathing. Such deep breathing is easy and natural when one's posture is correct. One deep breath between major pauses, with smaller, "catch breaths" at natural breaks in the verbal line should keep adequate support under one's tone. Try never to feel short of breath toward the end of a sentence. If that happens, try one or more of several simple things. Try reading aloud more frequently in private. Part of the problem may be shallow breathing brought on by a touch of stage fright. Practice produces ease. Try standing erect, with the diaphragm tight. Take a deep breath and count slowly and aloud. See how many numbers it takes before there is too little breath to go on. If that is done several times a day, it will inevitably build up lung capacity and breath control.

Another major element in tone production is pitch. The higher the pitch of the voice, the more air is needed to keep the voice box vibrating, since the vibrations must be faster. The lower the pitch, the more support the column of air needs, because it is being released more slowly. A medium pitch within the normal range will use the air supply the most efficiently. It is easiest to use one's normal speaking pitch. It is the most comfortable, and the one to which one's tone-production equipment is most habituated.

For speaking purposes, consider a word to be made up of vowel sounds that are cut off and divided by consonants. The sounds that carry and are heard are the vowels. The sounds that distinguish one vowel from another and make the word intelligible are the consonants. To make the word audible, therefore, the vowels must project clearly. To make the word intelligible, the consonants must be crisp and distinguishable.

Projecting a vowel sound is primarily a question of placement. The further forward in the head and the more rounded the lips during the production of the vowel sound, the more clearly it will project. For example, pronounce "alleluia," with all its vowels; first with one's lips nearly in a smiling position. Listen to the "a" sound. Then produce just that "a." Continue to make that sound while moving the lips more nearly into a circle. Listen for the difference in the "a" sound as it is transformed by the lip movement. Then try projecting several of the possible "a" sounds that have been produced, speaking as loudly as possible. The rounder the lips, the further the projection. A reading tone should be as round as the proper pronunciation of the words will allow.

For speaking purposes, consonants serve three purposes: they initiate words; they divide syllables; they end words and separate them from their neighbors. Most consonants, as long as they are pronounced clearly, provide a minimum of difficulty. Some, however, especially as initiating or terminal consonants, need to be watched carefully. There are the "sharp" consonants: b, c/k, d, p, t. If not pronounced with care, they tend to disappear.

The larger the building, or the greater its capacity for echo, the more important it is to be sure that the consonants really do divide words. Words run together in a large building become unintelligible. For this reason, carefully pronounced consonants are essential.

As a general rule, all public reading should be slower than normal speech patterns, unless those patterns are unusually slow. The auditor is hearing language and ideas that are not "everyday" in nature or content. They are, moreover, words of particular importance. It is to be hoped that those listening are listening carefully. Careful listening is aided by deliberately paced reading. That is a function of carefully projected vowels and crisp, cleanly pronounced consonants.

Until one is sure of one's pace in reading, it might be well to have someone else listen to a passage being read, and report at what pace the language was most easily heard. Then, practice at that pace until it becomes second nature.

The proper emphasis on the various words within a sentence is derived from the role that the individual words and phrases play within the structure of the sentence. It is particularly important to recognize this when dealing with the older forms, where the structure of the sentence is more apt to be unfamiliar to contemporary ears. If one can recognize how the various parts interrelate, however, reading with appropriate emphasis becomes easier.

No matter how long or complicated a sentence becomes, it has three benchmarks to which everything must relate: the subject, the verb and the complement. It is probably easiest to start out by looking for the person, pronoun (I, you, he, she, it, we, they) or thing who does whatever is done in the sentence. The subject often is very near the beginning of the sentence. When that is found, the word that describes what the subject does, or some form of the verb "to be" can be found. Then the person, pronoun, or thing to whom this action is done can be found. If the verb is some form of "to be," then look for a person, pronoun or thing which is the same as the subject. In a sentence the verb "to be" acts as an equal sign. Everything else in the sentence must, in one way or another, further define, describe or delineate the subject, the verb or the complement. In many cases, particularly in the older forms, this additional material is interspersed among the three basic parts of the sentence. That is less true in contemporary rites and translations. It is this complex separation that, in fact, gives the "churchy" flavor to the older forms. Such a style was the literary norm of the period, and was based upon Greek and Latin models.

In some cases, if the action of the sentence is not direct (or active), but indirect (passive), there will be no direct object. For example, an active verb would occur in a sentence that went, "God helped me." In a sentence, "I was helped by God," the verb is passive and there is no direct object. The latter is less usual, however.

In sum, then, look for the subject and the verb. Unless the latter is "to be" or passive, look for the object. If it is "to be," look for the complement that is the same as the subject. If it is passive, look for the agent of the action, which will serve the purpose of making a complete thought. Then try to find what parts of the sentence further define each. When that is done, the structure of the sentence will be clear. It is then possible to emphasize the main words most, and relate the rest to each other by appropriate tone of voice.

There are several common pitfalls in public reading. One common one is to emphasize the preposition in a prepositional phrase. They are those small words like to, for, after, and among, which, with a noun, tend to define time or place. They are always followed by a noun. Only in the rarest of circumstances is the preposition emphasized. It is always the noun which receives the emphasis. Yet, far too often, one hears the reading the other way.

In the Scriptures there is an abnormally large number of "and's." Quite often one finds these, too, being emphasized. In classical times punctuation had not been invented, so the word "and" was ordinarily used much as we would use a comma nowadays. Since sentences tended to be longer and more complex than modern style calls for, the conjunction "and" is extremely common. It is also of less importance than it is in contemporary writing.

At all times, but especially until one is used to the discipline of reading aloud, as well as to the particular place in which that reading is to be done, it is best to have someone monitor practice sessions and make suggestions. This is also helpful from time to time after one has become an "old pro" at the practice.

If one has problems, the local high school speech teacher or drama coach will probably be glad to help. The matter is central to one's responsibilities as a lay reader. The accuracy and propriety with which the reading is done is an essential matter.[2]

2. Clifford W. Atkinson, *A Lay Reader's Guide to the Book of Common Prayer* (Wilton, Conn.: Morehouse-Barlow Co., Inc., 1977), 79–84. Copyright © 1977 by Morehouse-Barlow Co., Inc.; reprinted by permission of the publisher.

GLOSSARY

Acolyte From the Greek for "to follow." A liturgical assistant to the ministers. The term includes such functions as crucifer, torchbearer, bannerbearer, and bookbearer.

Alb A full-length, white vestment with long sleeves, worn by worship leaders since the early sixth century.

Altar The table upon which the Holy Communion is celebrated. From the Latin for "high place."

Ambo A reading desk or lectern.

Antiphon A brief verse from the Psalms or other Scriptures which is sung or said before and after Psalms.

Assisting Minister A person (usually but not always a lay person) who assists in leading worship, reading lessons, leading intercessions, and distributing Communion.

Aumbry A small cupboard on the wall of the chancel or sacristy in which consecrated eucharistic elements may be kept.

Baptistery A section of the church building where Baptisms take place.

Burse A square case used to store the corporal, the post-Communion veil, and the purificators for the Holy Communion. It is also used to carry these items to and from the altar.

Cantor An assisting minister who leads liturgical singing.

Cassock A long, black garment worn by worship leaders.

Censer See Thurible.

Cerecloth A cloth, cut the same dimensions as the mensa; ususally treated with wax. It is the first cloth placed upon an altar and is covered by the fair linen.

Chalice The cup used in administering the wine in the Holy Communion.

Chancel The area of the church building where the altar and pulpit are located.

Chasuble A poncho-like vestment worn by the presiding minister (who is always ordained) at a celebration of Holy Communion.

Ciborium A covered, chalice-like vessel containing wafers for Holy Communion.

Cincture A cloth, rope-like belt which is worn with the alb.

Communion Stations The distribution of Holy Communion at convenient places within the church, such as at the head of each aisle, at which communicants receive while standing. Particularly useful for large gatherings.

Compline See Prayer at the Close of the Day.

Cope A cape-like vestment worn by worship leaders for processions and certain festive occasions.

Corporal A square, white, linen cloth (carried in the burse) which is unfolded and placed on the center of the altar. The vessels used for Holy Communion are then placed on it.

Cotta A short, white garment with wide sleeves, worn over the cassock by musicians, acolytes, and assisting ministers.

Credence A table or shelf near the altar holding the vessels for the Holy Communion.

Crucifer One who carries the cross in a procession.

Cruet A glass vessel which holds wine needed for Communion.

Daily Prayer Prayer offices of Morning Prayer, Evening Prayer, and Prayer at the Close of the Day.

Entrance Hymn The opening hymn in the Holy Communion liturgy.

Eucharist A name for the Holy Communion; from the Greek for "thanksgiving."

Evening Prayer The evening service of prayer (also known as Vespers).

Fair Linen The top, white, linen cloth covering an altar.

Flagon A vessel which holds the wine needed for Communion.

Font A pool or large basin which holds water for Holy Baptism. The word means "fountain" or "spring."

Frontal A covering which hangs over the front of the altar. A superfrontal, or short cover, may be used as an additional hanging over the frontal.

Gospel Procession Procession in which the Bible is carried into the midst of the congregation for the reading of the Gospel, symbolizing Christ coming into the midst of his people.

Great Thanksgiving The section of the Holy Communion liturgy including the Preface Dialog, Proper Preface, Sanctus, Prayer of Thanksgiving, and the Lord's Prayer.

Incense A mixture of spices for ceremonial burning, symbolizing prayer and purification. One of the gifts of the magi to Jesus.

Intercessor The assisting minister who leads in intercessory prayer.

Lectern A desk to hold the Bible or lectionary for public reading.

Lectionary A schedule of lessons from the Holy Scriptures for the Sundays and festivals of the church year. (Series A, B, and C comprise the three-year lectionary.) Also refers to the book containing those lessons.

Lector The assisting minister who reads the lessons.

Liturgy The prescribed worship service of the church, especially the Holy Communion. From the Greek for "people's work."

Matins See Morning Prayer.

Mensa The top surface of the altar.

Missal The *Ministers Edition* of the LBW, used at the altar to lead worship (also known as altar book).

Missal Stand The stand on which the altar service book rests. When not in use at the altar, it is placed on the credence.

Morning Prayer The morning service of praise and prayer (also known as Matins).

Narthex The entrance hall of the church building.

Nave The section of a church building where the congregation assembles for worship.

Offertory Procession The act of bringing the bread, wine, and money offerings to the altar.

Orans Traditional biblical posture for leading prayer, in which the hands are uplifted and outstretched. From the Latin for "prayer."

Pall A small, linen-covered square used to cover the chalice (while it is not in use) during Holy Communion.

Paraments Cloth hangings used on the altar and pulpit. Their color is that of the liturgical season or day. Altar hangings are called frontals; pulpit hangings are called antependia.

Paschal Candle A large candle placed on the Gospel side of chancel (the congregation's left) from Easter Eve through the Day of Pentecost. It symbolizes our Lord's resurrection. After the Easter season, this candle is placed near the font and is lighted for each Baptism. For funerals, it is placed at the head of the coffin.

Paten A plate which holds the bread for distribution during Holy Communion.

Peace, Exchange of A time in the liturgy when worshipers greet each other with a sign of baptismal unity, reconciliation, and peace, such as a handclasp or embrace (Romans 16:16).

Piscina A basin in the sacristy which drains directly into the ground; used for the disposal of baptismal water and the wine which remains in the chalice after the Eucharist.

Prayer at the Close of the Day The late evening service of prayer (also known as Compline).

Predella The altar platform on which the presiding minister stands when celebrating the Holy Communion.

Presiding Minister The ordained pastor who presides in the celebration of the liturgy.

Processional Cross A cross on a staff carried at the head of a procession.

Propers The changeable parts of the liturgy which are different for each day: Psalm, lessons, Prayer of the Day, Hymn of the Day, appointed Verse, appointed Offertory, and Proper Preface.

Pulpit The raised platform for public speaking where the sermon is delivered.

Purificator A small, square, linen cloth used to cleanse the chalice during the administration of Holy Communion.

Pyx Short, covered container containing wafers for Holy Communion.

Responsive Prayer Liturgical prayer service of versicles and responses (also known as Suffrages).

Rubric A rule or direction for the proper conduct of worship. Rubrics are usually printed in red.

Sacristy The room used for storing vestments, paraments, sacramental vessels, and other items used in worship. Also used as a vesting room.

Sanctuary That part of the chancel where the altar is located.

Sedilia The seats in the chancel area for clergy, assisting ministers, and acolytes.

Sign of the Cross Tracing the outline of the cross with the hand as a remembrance of Baptism and a mark of unity with the crucified Lord.

Stole A cloth band worn by ordained pastors around the neck and hanging to the knees, in the liturgical color of the day or season; a symbol of ordination.

Surplice A white, full-sleeved vestment worn over the cassock.

Thurible The vessel in which incense is burned (also called censer).

Thurifer The one who carries the censer (or thurible) containing the burning incense.

Torches Large candles attached to wooden or metal staffs, carried in processions.

Vespers See Evening Prayer.

Vestments The distinctive garb worn during the various services of the church by presiding and assisting ministers, musicians, and acolytes.

BIBLIOGRAPHY

Allen, Horace T., Jr., ed. *The Reader as Minister.* Washington: The Liturgical Conference, 1980. Suggestions for establishing a lector program and training lectors.

Bauman, William. *The Ministry of Music.* Rev. ed. Washington: The Liturgical Conference, 1979. Includes chapter of practical guidance for cantors.

Brand, Eugene L., and S. Anita Stauffer. *By Water and the Spirit.* Philadelphia: Parish Life Press, 1979. Study resource on the LBW liturgy for Holy Baptism, with accompanying pastor's guide.

Davies, J. G., ed. *The New Westminster Dictionary of Liturgy and Worship.* Philadelphia: Westminster Press, 1986. A dictionary of liturgical terms.

Harrison, G. B., and John McCabe. *Proclaiming the Word.* New York: Pueblo Publishing Company, 1973. Practical handbook for lectors.

Lonergan, Ray. *A Well-Trained Tongue.* Chicago: Liturgy Training Publications, 1982. Workbook for lectors' use in preparing to read.

Lutheran Book of Worship. Minneapolis: Augsburg Publishing House; Philadelphia: Board of Publication, LCA, 1978. Authorized worship book, containing liturgies, Psalms, and hymns.

Lutheran Book of Worship Ministers Edition. Minneapolis: Augsburg Publishing House; Philadelphia: Board of Publication, LCA, 1978. Authorized leaders' edition of the LBW; contains additional liturgical texts and complete rubrics.

Nitschke, Beverley A., and Stephen D. Swenson. *With This Bread and Cup.* Philadelphia: Parish Life Press, 1985. Study resource on the LBW Holy Communion liturgy, with accompanying pastor's guide.

Occasional Services. Minneapolis: Augsburg Publishing House; Philadelphia: Board of Publication, LCA, 1982. Authorized auxiliary collection of rites for installations, dedications, ministry to the sick, etc.

Petrich, Roger T. *Psalm Antiphons for the Church Year.* Philadelphia: Fortress Press, 1979. Musical settings of the Psalm antiphons from the LBW.

Pfatteicher, Philip H. *Distributing Communion to the Sick and Homebound.* Minneapolis: Augsburg Publishing House; Philadelphia: Board of Publication, LCA, 1982. Guide for lay ministers, with accompanying pastor's training guide.

Pfatteicher, Philip H. *In Love and Faithfulness.* Philadelphia: Parish Life Press, 1982. Study resource on the LBW marriage liturgy, with accompanying pastor's guide.

Pfatteicher, Philip H., and Carlos R. Messerli. *Manual on the Liturgy: Lutheran Book of Worship.* Minneapolis: Augsburg Publishing House, 1979. Practical manual on leading the liturgies in the LBW.

Reed, Luther D. *The Lutheran Liturgy.* Rev. ed. Philadelphia: Fortress Press, 1960. History of and commentary on the liturgy.

Stauffer, S. Anita. *Altar Guild Handbook.* Philadelphia: Fortress Press, 1985. Complete guide to the worship space and its furnishings.

Stauffer, S. Anita, ed. *Communion Practices Study Guide.* Minneapolis: Augsburg Publishing House; Philadelphia: Fortress Press, 1980. Commentary on the 1978 ALC-LCA Statement on Communion Practices.

Stauffer, S. Anita. *Lutherans at Worship.* Minneapolis: Augsburg Publishing House; Philadelphia: Board of Publication, LCA, 1978. An introduction to the LBW, with accompanying leader's guide.

Van Loon, Ralph R. *Space for Worship.* Rev. ed. Philadelphia: Division for Parish Services, LCA, 1982. Practical guide to the worship space and its furnishings.

Van Loon, Ralph R. *Parish Worship Handbook.* Philadelphia: Parish Life Press, 1979. Helpful guide to planning and leading parish worship.